JUST ANOTHER PILGRIM ON THE TRUCK TO LEH

CHICK LEWIS

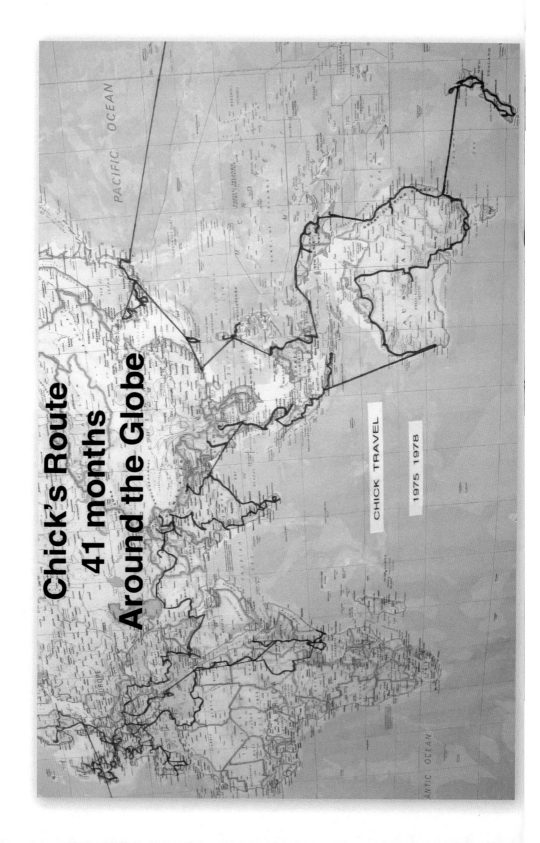

JUST ANOTHER PILGRIM ON THE TRUCK TO LEH

Chick Lewis' Vagabonding Tales through Europe, the Middle East, & Asia

1975-76

Published by Lewis/Heaton Publications

First Edition

Cover design by Backus Studio

Book interior and ebook produced by Booknook.biz

ISBN 979-8-87207588-2 (paperback)

*This work is dedicated to **Matt Lewis**, my brother, and the best male human I know. Whenever life has me feeling boxed-in, a generous dose of Matt's Sane, Upbeat World-View always unsticks me, and gets me back on track. It is a privilege to be related to the guy.*

Contents

Mideast Maneuvers   **67**

Contents

About the Author

Chick Lewis is likely one of the most widely-traveled guys you've met, having visited 140 of the qualifying "countries and island groups" on the 'Traveler's Century Club' list.

In January 1975, at the age of 24, Chick gave notice to his job as a physicist, sold nearly everything he owned, and headed out from Los Angles with $5900 of savings to see the world. And see it he did. In the following 41 months of Super-Low-Budget Vagabonding, he used the cheapest local transport, stretched every dollar, and opened himself up to the beauty of the people and cultures—and adventures—surrounding him, as he circumnavigated the globe.

During this 3-and-a-half-year-long journey, Chick roamed through 60 sovereign nations, seeking out numerous remote, exotic, and often ill-advised locations, some of which are only accessible to the very most determined travelers today. In this book, *Just Another Pilgrim on the Truck to Leh*, are the 16 months of his experiences in Europe, the Middle East, and Asia. These range from meeting amazingly generous and good-hearted people to dealing with phenomenally nasty scammers, thieves, crooked police, corrupt officials, and-ne'er-do-wells.

If we include his journeys through Africa and the Far East, Chick survived quite a number of life-threatening experiences, such as a Fatal Auto Accident, Dysentery, Gangrene, Malaria, Hepatitis, and Dengue Fever, very nearly drowning, a serious tribal fight, and a bandit ambush, making Chick probably also the *luckiest* guy you've ever met.

Returning home after vagabonding, Chick was invited to be first employee of 3D Systems, the company which invented 3D printing. He designed and built the prototypes for the world's first commercial 3-D printers, using resin and lasers, and is named as a co-inventor on at least 18 US Patents. Chick retired in 2009 and resumed traveling extensively.

This memoir/travelogue, *Just Another Pilgrim on the Truck to Leh*, is volume 2 of a 3 part series. It follows *Just Another Pilgrim on the Train to Wau*. A third book *Just Another Pilgrim on the Boat to Wewak* will continue where this one leaves off, including Southeast Asia, Australia, Oceania, and the Far East.

Chick's Credo for Vagabonding

Mental Preparation Before You Go:

1. Firstly, You must Believe Deeply and Sincerely that you are **JUST ANOTHER DOOFUS**, nobody important or special. All of life made much more sense to me after I fully internalized this fact. Makes it much harder to feel that you are persecuted or unlucky in any current circumstance.

2. Convince yourself that you will be Sick Often, so that you won't become discouraged when it happens.

3. For all of the things you plan to take along, convince yourself that you will **LOSE THEM ALL**, at least Twice, and get comfortable with that idea. Anything irreplaceable and precious to you, leave it at home.

4. Know that the language barrier will never prevent communication IF you can find someone who is willing to TRY to understand you. Gestures and a few words, if enthusiastically listened to, will always suffice.

After the Launch:

In **Chick's Credo for Vagabonding** one:

- Travels to a new place using local transport,
- Stays in the cheapest available lodging,
- Interacts with the local people,
- Learns twenty words of the local language,
- Eats the local foods,
- Samples the local diseases,
- Experiences the local cultural ceremonies,
- Tries out the local intoxicants,
- then Decides whether to move on, or to stay awhile longer.

General and Specific Advice:

Your attitude is crucially important. Unsophisticated people's attitude towards you will 'mirror' your attitude towards them. If you are feeling grouchy and closed-down and mean, then you will have a lousy response. If you remain open and friendly and engaging, they will treat you in the same fashion.

Always exhibit confidence. Even if you are lost and alone and worried, you CANNOT allow these feelings to show. They will attract human predators like moths to an arc-light. Always pretend that you are comfortable, exactly where you want to be, and that your plans are moving forward.

Leave maximum flexibility for schedule changes and re-routing. As much as possible, avoid committing to future "hard" dates when you must be somewhere or do something.

Pick a backpack narrow enough that while wearing it, you still fit through a bus doorway.

When crossing borders overland, never buy passage across a border, nor cross as part of a group with folks who you do not know extremely well and COMPLETELY trust. Arrive at the border, detach from everyone, cross the border with your belongings, and find transport again on the far side of the border.

Remember the primary rule of overland travel in the Middle East and Asia:

> **"In any interaction, a little BAKSHEESH (small bribe or tip) smooths the path."**

Note on the Images

Most of the included images are my photographs, taken with a small, viewfinder Canon camera on Ektachrome color slide film. You may note that many of them which include people are taken from behind or to the side of them. I'm very sensitive to the shyness of local people, and have always felt that pointing a camera at someone, especially an unsophisticated person, is like dropping a barrier between you. It seems like treating them as objects rather than humans whom you honor and respect. Others of the images were taken by my traveling companion Linda Hill, who carried a Single-Lens-Reflex camera which could do closeups at long range. Those are identified in the captions.

Introduction

Just Another Pilgrim on the Truck to Leh

What interests Chick—History, Culture, Archaeology, Warfare, Architecture, Bridges, Geology

So, how did I decide to go vagabonding in 1975-78? When I was ten years old I remember telling Walt, my father, that I wanted to go traveling around the world. I announced that reading about the Great Pyramid sitting there in California wasn't as good as reading about the great pyramid while sitting on top of it. Similarly, actually seeing Mount Everest by moonlight must be superior to reading about the Himalayas. My father, of course, thought that my plan was a bad one, as it could put me at great risk. But Walt was smart, and realized that to discourage or try to forbid my vagabonding plan might increase the probability that it would occur.

"That is a great idea", said Walt, "but you should continue in school and get good grades, then get into the university, earn a degree which leads to a lucrative job, use that job to earn money and THEN go vagabonding."

He figured, naturally, that by the time this all played through I would be married, with a wife and a mortgage, and other responsibilities, and that the whole idea would never even reach the serious-planning stage.

I followed his suggestions IN EVERY DETAIL. In late 1974 I had managed to save up $6900 USD and was in process of selling off nearly all of my worldly possessions.

In this volume you will not find many tales of visiting the famous major tourist attractions. I viewed them just like every other tourist, but you can find such stories in plenty of other places. I intend, rather, to concentrate upon the more off-beat and unusual sites and sights. Interesting interactions with people, unusual situations, and anything which makes a "Good Story" is more likely to be included.

I trust this travelogue will be of some interest.

Chick Lewis

The Tale so far—

January of 1975, I flew to Munich and hitch-hiked down through Austria and Italy, seeing all the obligatory sights. I continued south, visiting Sicily, then across the Mediterranean to Tunisia in North Africa. Hitching across Libya to Egypt, I then headed south up the Nile to The Sudan, Uganda, Kenya, Tanzania, and Ethiopia, gathering adventures along the way. If that route interests you, the reader, you will very likely enjoy the previous volume of my vagabonding travels:

Just another Pilgrim on the Train to Wau

available through Amazon in electronic as well as paperback formats.

Loose in Europe

Leaving Africa after 5 months of super-low-budget vagabonding I landed in Athens and immediately took a tram to the Acropolis, which was very photogenic and interesting. The Dapne wine festival was in full swing, and fun to visit. I sought out the Greek War Museum, which was fascinating, but none of the exhibits were in any language other than Greek, which I cannot read.

The youth hostel in Athens was modern and slick, and included a trendy café. Sitting there at a table with two Australians chatting, a fourth young man approached and sat with us. Standard introductions were made. I'm Kevin from Nebraska. I'm Chick from California. We are Hal and Mike from Australia. Kevin considered this carefully, then asked how long ago the Australians had left home. When informed that it had only been a month, he opined "A month, eh, well, you picked up English awfully quickly." Both Australians' heads snapped immediately to me, impeached by the astonishing cluelessness of my Nebraskan compatriot. I had nowhere to hide from their wry amusement. Maybe Kevin confused Australia with Austria?

Abandoning Athens I hitched past the amazing Corinth canal, and photographed some "Tholos" tombs, which had a 'beehive' shape. They boggled me as they are clearly the intermediary design in the development of the architectural arch. Knowing that flat 'lintel' stones sometimes break, the Tholos tomb architects designed a 'relieving triangle' above the lintel. This worked well, but some bright bulb must have realized that this change made the lintel itself redundant, and removed it from the next design, leading to the true arch.

Tholos Tomb

Mycenae

Mycenae was the location of Schliemann's discovery of what he believed to be King Agamemnon's treasure, and the Lion Gate, the earliest monumental sculpture found in Greece. The youth hostel there was big, and modern, and VERY full in the summertime, but after all the beds had been claimed, it was still permitted to sleep on the flat concrete roof. forty or fifty 'Euro Youth' sat there in the warm Grecian night. Guitars were played and travel stories told. The "I can top that" story competition ended convincingly with my tale of being chased by serious spear-throwing Shilluk tribesmen in the Sudan. Those assembled then decided that it was time to sleep.

One gal asked me where I was sleeping. I admitted that my sleeping bag was laid out over there, whereupon she patted the empty space on the concrete beside her, the second-most-direct romantic come-on I have ever enjoyed.

4

If the story of riding on top of a train across the deserts of Sudan and being chased by Shilluk spear-throwers is interesting to you, please check out the previous volume of my vagabonding travels in *Just Another Pilgrim on the Train to Wau*, available on Amazon, Kindle, and in Paperback.

New friend Victoria hailed from Brick Town New Jersey and was knocking around Greece for the summer. She had heritage connections and friends in the country, and spoke a bit of Greek. In the morning we returned to the Mycenae excavations and explored two big rock-hewn cisterns. Through poor planning, I didn't have the luxury of my flashlight.

Having Vic along was an advantage in hitch-hiking because male Greek drivers stopped for her as though she were pointing a loaded pistol at them. But some just couldn't seem to keep their grubby hands off of her, and I was occasionally called upon to quietly threaten mayhem. That generally convinced "Macho, Gurgling Greek men" (Victoria's unflattering category) to show her more respect.

At the quaint seaside town of Nafplion we found a backpacker beach with fig and orange trees, plus ripe cactus apples, in the area immediately behind the sand. The water was very nice, and the weather was merely perfect. Every morning we would walk the mile into town and buy our daily food and a bottle of cheap Retsina. That beverage is a pine-pitch-flavored white wine for which I developed a fondness. To this day Retsina always tastes to me like snuggling on the beach in the summer night.

The seawater behaved strangely as it contained a few big, bright scattered phosphorescent plankton which gleamed with intense brief light when the water was disturbed. They could be seen at night, and it was like swimming in a dark ocean with twinkling stars.

Together we hitched to see convent Agia Moni. Victoria bathed briefly in the legendary fountain in which the Goddess Hera renewed her virginity every year.

The quiet, slow-paced seaside town of Nea Epidavros was our next destination, and easily reached. We dropped our backpacks in a roadside stubble field, confident that they would not be interfered with before our return to sleep. In the reconstructed Greek theatre at the Sanctuary of Asclepius, the ancient play Lysistrata was performed using the oldest version of the script. Although I couldn't understand the words, it seemed to be a very 'raunchy' play. We walked back to our backpacks and slept with our heads against a lone olive tree.

Shady Briefcase

In the early morning I awakened to the sound of an auto engine. Rolling over I could see the rear view of a black Mercedes about 50 yards away, just sitting in the field with engine idling. Hmmm, that seemed strange. Unusually ugly chickens surrounded us watching intently. Then the rear door opened and a guy wearing a dark suit got out, walked into 'our' field, picked up a black briefcase, and returned to the car. Yowee, now I really hoped they would not spot us, as they were certainly up to something for which witnesses would not be welcome. When the Mercedes drove off without spotting our sleeping bags, I felt relief.

We had a scare later that morning. Standing beside the road a BIG long, heavy plank used for scaffolding slid off of the load of a passing truck and simply smashed through Victoria's bedroll which was lying immediately at her feet!! A few inches higher and she would inevitably have been crippled. Our rides that day caried us to Olympia, where the hostel provided the first showers and real beds we had enjoyed for a few weeks.

Vic had family in Sparta. Ruins there were very sparse, as the Spartans never built defensive walls. When I was introduced, Victoria's distant cousins gave me serious 'stink-eye', so I headed out on my own, leaving her safe in their hands.

Before long I was charmed by the reassembled pieces of the "Navel of the World" sculpture at Delphi. In ancient times Delphi was considered the center of the civilized world, and distances were often referenced to there. The Delphi Oracle was the most famous and revered of all ancient oracles. To me it was a place of pilgrimage.

To Macedonia

I was just about satisfied with my self-guided tour of mainland Greece. Poste Restante in Vienna was my next maildrop location and in the days before instant worldwide communications, mail from home was compellingly attractive. I awoke on the ground in the forest near Delphi. Displaying my California state flag and sticking out my thumb, I headed north towards Yugoslavia and Vienna, about 1000 miles away. Hitch hiking was just great. I went by truck to Itea, truck to Amfissa, car to Cordita, truck to nowhere in particular, car to Trikala, truck to Meteora, van to some nameless spot, truck to Grevena, same truck as took me to Meteora reappeared and carried me to Kozani, truck to nowhere, van to nowhere, car full of family to Florina, another car full of family to the Yugoslav border. I had been given 13 rides, all with Greeks—13 busy hours to travel more than 400 km.

Meteora

I viewed the wonderful rocky pinnacles of Meteora, Thermo-pylae pass, and what was probably Mount Olympus, wreathed in clouds. It was well after dark when I cleared the Macedonian border on foot and walked half a mile before crawling into an arched culvert under the road to sleep.

Sunday morning I crawled out, stiff and dirty, and was imme-diately picked up by a Yugoslav family in their best clothes on the way to church! Their charming four-year-old daughter in starched white lace quietly took my grubby hand and held it for the entire ride. A few additional short rides brought me to a campground on the shore of Lake Ohrid, with mysterious Alba-nia as the dim distant shore. After stealing a shower, I was soon adopted by 5 Yugoslav guys camped there, one of whom, Vasi, spoke fluent English. We visited a club in the nearest town that evening before crashing in their tents.

Gallic Rejection!

Monday morning a vision appeared in the campsite just across the way. Two camping vans with French registrations were in residence, and those two couples had between them 6 attractive teen-aged daughters. We youngsters were all clearly aware of one another. Vasi suggested: "You speak French, Chick, go over there and bring those girls back here and introduce us." I agreed to try, grabbing the final ⅓rd of a watermelon as an opening gambit. As I headed across the byway, the gals saw me coming and smiled. One of the French fathers moved purposefully to intercept me.

Chick (in French): "We have eaten all we want of this, would you like to have the remainder?"
French Father: shakes his head NO.

Chick: "No, truly we wish to give it to you, please accept this small gift."

French Father, dismissively: "Only North Africans eat that." And turning on his heel, he walked back to his vehicle.

—I crawled back to my new buddies, horribly defeated!

Battered in Bosnia

The following morning I caught an excellent ride in a Volkswagen bug piloted by a German guy named Peter Fink. We drove together all afternoon before settling down to rough-camp beside the car in a cow pasture about 90 km before Titograd. Upon arising we drove as part of a line of trucks on the one-lane-each-way mountain road. Peter would pull out around a truck to check if it was safe to pass, then pull back behind the truck if vehicles came the other way. After 20 minutes of this stressful driving he again made a move around the truck immediately ahead to see a bus approaching us from the other direction. He had plenty of time to drop back into our own lane, and I had time to think—Oh, he'll pull back now—Well, time to drop back—but he did not, nor did he brake. We hit the bus head-on at decent speed!

WHAM!!

and I was knocked mostly senseless. The Volkswagen had no seat belts, so I smashed forward catching the top of my head on the frame of the windshield, shattering the glass with my cheekbone, then bouncing back forcefully enough to actually rip the passenger seat off of its mounting! This meant that I was lying on my back as we mashed in under the front of the bus, while Peter was sitting up still gripping the wheel. I was on 'autopilot', but functioning, and recall only a few flashes of lucidity. I remember many folks looking horrified out of the bus side windows. I remember pulling my backpack out of the back seat and leaning it up against the mountain wall. I remember seeing Peter behind the steering wheel grimacing as people tried to pry him out of the wreck. There was yet another problem. The gas tank on an old VW bug is just above the passenger's feet, and had been ruptured. I was soaked in a generous marinade of both blood and gasoline! Luckily Peter didn't smoke, and neither did I, so we were not immediately immolated.

When I finally came back to full consciousness, I found myself in the back seat of a small auto with the driver's wife looking back very worriedly at me. I had really no clue even what country I was in, but my first priority was to reassure the poor stressed-out gal. One thing was somehow clear to me:

"I'm gonna be ok, don't worry, I'm not gonna die."

I discovered that I was soaked in both gasoline and blood, and my left hand didn't work at all so I must have been in an auto accident. Over the next few minutes I sorted things out and remembered I was in Bosnia, and had been riding with Peter Fink before he inexplicably caused a nasty collision. After 15 minutes or so the nice couple delivered me to the biggest hospital in Titograd.

I walked myself into the hospital, which in retrospect was a mistake, because for the next three hours they had me up and walking all over the facility as I got woozier and woozier. In any US hospital, the first thing staff does with an injured person is slap them into a wheelchair or onto a gurney. Finally while climbing another flight of stairs I just turned around and sat down rather than faint. A wheelchair was fetched for me.

Before launching on my vagabonding trip my housemate had given me what he called the 'magic traveling bangle'. It was "C"-shaped, heavy, made of light-colored brass, and it was said to provide some unspecified protection to travelers. I wore it always on my left wrist, but after the collision I realized that it had vanished. Hmmmm, curious.

Playing 'Telephone'

We had communication problems. NOBODY on the hospital staff spoke either English or French. An intern named Gojko spoke German, but my 40 words of pidgin German were not sufficient. A policeman appeared who spoke Italian, but again, my 40 words of Italian were inadequate. Someone had the excellent idea of walking us all to the other end of the hospital where a Dutch woman was recovering from an auto crash. Once there the cop told the intern in Bosnian, who told the Dutch gal in German, who told me in English, and we played this game of back and forth. I was giving them exactly the answer they wanted to hear; that the collision was caused by Peter. So the cop asked me to write up everything I remembered, with positional diagrams, in English, sign it, and he would be back sometime to pick up my statement. That sounded ok, EXCEPT the police officer disappeared with my passport, which is not a good situation. I really felt vulnerable any time that passport wasn't within a quarter inch of my skin.

Now with the paperwork out of the way, hospital staff finally decided to get my injuries cleaned up and treated. Nurses washed

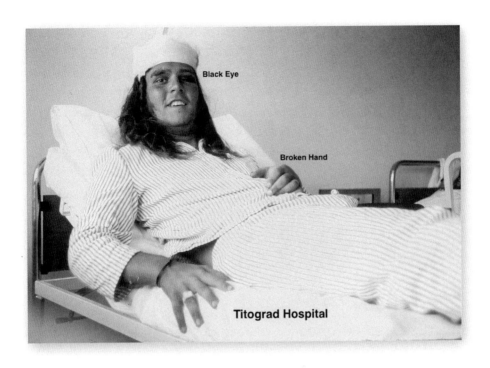

Black Eye

Broken Hand

Titograd Hospital

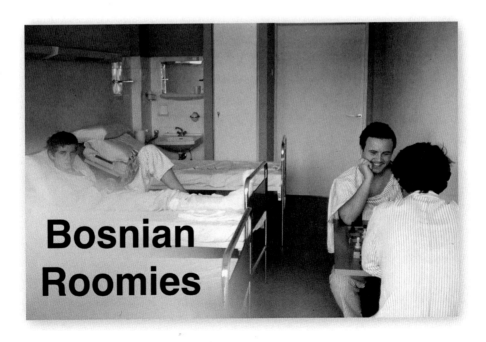

Bosnian
Roomies

off the blood and picked some glass shards out of me. A big bald patch was shaved just above my forehead and butterfly bandages were used to pull the edges of my split scalp back together. When X-rays were taken, metacarpal bones of the ring and middle fingers of my left hand displayed very sharp shattered ends from diagonal fractures. We also discovered 2 broken ribs up under my left arm. My head was bandaged and my left hand wrapped before I was deposited in the window bed of a three-bed ward. Personable Bosnian guys occupied the other two places.

Tweezers

But there were still problems, as I could feel plenty of razor-sharp chunks of safety glass remaining embedded in my shoulder and arm. I tried to explain to the nurses, using sign language, that there were shards which had not been removed, pointing to the injuries and even drawing a picture of a pair of tweezers, but they blithely refused to even try to understand me. Therefore I took matters into my own hands. I climbed the stairs to the upper floor, searched out the treatment room, shut myself inside, opened drawers until I found tweezers, turned on one of the powerful examination lamps, and sat there in front of an articulated mirror pulling jagged fragments out of my skin. There was considerable commotion when a nurse discovered me there, but it did trigger a second attempt to locate and remove embedded glass. Since that day, every ten years or so, small shards of auto glass 'heal out' of my skin, and today I can locate one still under the skin near my elbow. The need to FORCE the staff to properly treat my injuries was another indication that I was ultimately 'on my own' in Titograd hospital. Nobody was watching out for me.

Before 'lights out' I visited Peter still on a gurney in the emergency room, attached to an IV. He was full of drugs and I couldn't get him to respond to anything I said or did. Peter really didn't look well at all, he was pale, and his feet and calves were cold.

In the morning, various somber-looking staff came around to tell me that overnight Peter had died. That was sobering. There are only a few inches between the front seats of a VW bug, and the odds against one passenger being killed while the other actually walks away from the carnage are very long.

I wrote a long aerogram message to Peter Fink's family recording all the details of his passing and paid to have it posted to them. If they sent any response it never caught up with me.

Solving Hospital Hunger

Food was also a bit of an issue. Meals were very boring, and portions quite skimpy. First dinner had been soggy cabbage, tomato, an egg, and a tiny sausage. Breakfast was a piece of bread and a morsel of goat cheese. Lunch was mashed potatoes, a goat fragment, tomato and bread. Dinner was rice stew and some bread with a dab of processed cheese. So, at about 2 am of my 2nd night, I got out of bed and walked downstairs searching to the other end of the hospital before finding the kitchen, dark and quiet. Lights on and a short additional hunt turned up leftover sausages and hardboiled eggs. I ate my fill of those. It seems that the Bosnians are such reliable rule-followers that no systems were in place to prevent people like me from breaking the rules. Midnight requisition of leftover food became part of my nightly routine, and I was never caught.

A few days later, while visiting folks downstairs, I blundered into the staff lounge. Before being sent away I noticed that real cheese and sausages were being consumed in great quantity there, explaining the dearth of food for the patients. Seemed to be a perfect demonstration of "Me First" Socialism.

"Signaturo"

I did manage to write up a statement of everything that I knew about the collision, including diagrams. When the Italian-speaking police officer returned I gave it to him. He pointed to the bottom margin and imperiously demanded: "Signaturo!" I had not signed the statement. I put out my empty broken left hand patting it and told him "Si, si, Passaporto → Signaturo!!" The cop cussed me out in several languages, shaking his finger at me, but I was adamant. To his displeasure and my delight, he returned the next day with my passport and traded it for my signature on the statement. I was very relieved to have the passport back, it would have been a massive hassle trying to find and retrieve it from the police files. I subsequently kept my passport in my skivvies, day and night.

Brain Damage?

I was slightly worried that my brain had been damaged by the huge knock my head had survived. And, how could I ever tell if my intellectual facilities had diminished? I had lots of time on my hands, and remembered that magic number squares were really interesting. I thought deeply about magic number squares, eventually working out a system by which I could create magic number squares of almost any size, and totaling to almost any chosen number. That largely put to rest my fear that I had suffered significant brain damage.

Failure to Tease

The large, evil-visaged head nurse on the day shift was named Beba. 'Sistra Beba' reeeeeally didn't like my long hair, and caught it up, pretending to use her fingers as scissors to cut it off. I then playfully caught her earlobe and pretend to snip it off with my fingers. One late morning Sistra Beba appeared at the doorway with two junior nurses, holding a tray covered by a towel. All three of them looked EXTREMELY pleased with themselves—definitely a danger sign! They approached on both sides of my bed, then dramatically whipped the towel away. On the tray were dozens of hair decorations, stretchies, beads, elastic bands, a tiara, colorful clip-ons, a mirror, a brush and a comb. The three then busily combed and brushed out my hair, catching it up a little bit at a time to add braiding and the various decorations. I had tufts sticking out in all directions, making me look completely ridiculous. Admiring their work in the hand-mirror, I thanked them apparently sincerely. They glanced at one another out of the corners of their eyes. My response was not the chagrined, embarrassed resistance they expected. So, unsatisfied, they disappeared. I sat in the bed reading and writing, apparently content with my ridiculous hairdo. Every hour Sistra Beba would march by in the hall and shoot me a quick look, finding that I hadn't taken down my hair. Finally she couldn't stand it any longer, and ten minutes before the end of her shift she returned to remove and carry off all of the hair decorations. I had out-psyched Sistra Beba for a clear victory.

"Fissura"

I was lobbying hard to be released from hospital, but it just wasn't happening. I knew that my only pair of pants had been split and shredded in the accident, and I would need something to wear when I was permitted to leave. My buddy Gojko the German-speaking intern somehow went outside the system so that my pants escaped temporarily from the secure lockup in the basement. With a needle and thread begged from the laundry-room ladies, I sewed up my pants so that they might keep me decent for a few hours of use.

Each late afternoon the doctor would stick his head into our doorway. I had been coached in Bosnian language by my room-mates, and I'd say "I want out of hospital" in that tongue. The doctor approached, shaking his head and tapped my skull, saying "Fis-

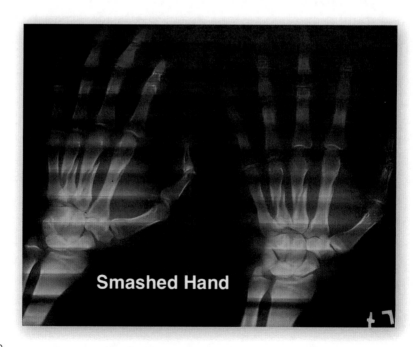

Smashed Hand

sura, Fissura" by which he clearly meant to say that I had a fractured skull. After the second such performance I got up in the middle of the night and went upstairs, inspecting each darkened room until I found the X-ray files. Searching there I discovered that my file listed me as 'Saputnik' meaning 'Wanderer', much like the Russian's first satellite. I turned on the light table and put my X-rays on it, looking hard at those of my skull. I'm not really trained to read x-rays, but had some experience from my summers working as an emergency-room orderly. Darned if I could see anything that looked like a 'Fissura'. I put everything back except the best X-ray of my broken hand, which I stole, and still possess today.

Next afternoon when the doctor appeared I had new words in Bosnian for him. "Radiographa—Here—Now" I said. Looking bemused he sent a nurse upstairs to bring my X-rays to him. When they arrived he took the skull X-rays over to the window and held them up to the light. "Oh—No Fissura—You can leave tomorrow morning!" The lazy guy had never actually seen my X-rays before, he had just believed the tech who had written notes in my file. In Titograd hospital I even had to read my own X-rays!!

Hospital Escape

Next morning the accounting staff calculated how much I owed the hospital for my week-long stay. It worked out to only $104 USD! They didn't want traveler's checks, so Gojko and I rode the bus to town, me dressed in slippers, my hospital gown, a borrowed bathrobe, with bandaged head and hand. Bringing the money back to the hospital, I tried to pay up. BUT of course, they had in the interim discovered additional charges and I owed them $161 USD instead. OK, back on the bus to the bank and while standing in line for the teller, just ahead of me was the nice man who had originally driven me to the hospital! We had a happy little reunion right there in the teller line. So, at only $161 dollars for seven nights plus medications plus X-rays plus treatments, the bill was SO inexpensive that I soon wrote my parents and had them cancel the medical insurance policy which I had been faithfully paying.

I had to sign for all of my belongings to get them out of the basement lockup. The system was determined to give me Peter's big, expensive single lens reflex camera, but I demanded that they ship it to Peter's next-of-kin. Very interestingly, my heavy brass traveling bangle (which I had worn non-stop during my vagabonding) reappeared, but horribly bent open and twisted around. I can't imagine how that might have happened, and it required a vise, a crowbar, and considerable strength to bend it back around to line up. I've always wondered if, when the killing impact arrived, the magic bangle had in some mysterious fashion absorbed the death blow for me, allowing me to undeservedly survive.

Out of Bosnia

Early evening I put on my backpack, walked straight out to the road in front of the hospital, and stuck out my thumb, again heading north towards the possibility of letters from home in Vienna. I soon discovered that it was quite difficult to deploy and re-pack my down sleeping bag with only one operational hand. Over the next day I passed Dubrovnik, Split, and Šibenik, on the way to Zadar. Hitch-hiking was much slower than it had been in Greece.

Reaching Ljubljana I paused to find a clinic which replaced the cast on my hand. Wandering around the center of that city I found that there were more unusually-beautiful women there than any other place I have ever visited. In most towns one woman in 20 might catch my attention as particularly attractive. In Ljubljana more than five in twenty captured my amorous eye!!

After a long day I found a railway cutting hideout and dropped off to sleep. I was awakened by the damp nose of a large German Shepherd dog. A gruff, uniformed guard was on the other end of the leash and indicated that I was to get lost. I laboriously packed up while he stayed to watch closely. Marching along the road for a mile offered no rides, so I went back to sleep beside the wire fence of a long-low factory building beside the road. I came half-awake, aware of heavy footsteps approaching on the gravel. They receded, but a few minutes later were again audible. A very kind security patrol officer had gone back to the factory, filled up a wine bottle with lovely clean water, and brought it back out to place it beside my head.

Austria

I finally crossed the border into Austria, and traveled on into Wien (Vienna) where I enjoyed seeing the famed Lipizzaner Stallions.

Several youth hostels surrounded Vienna, but I chose the one in Esterhazy Park, which was big and modern and air conditioned.

Salzburg was visited on my way to Germany and Munich, where I had stayed a year previously. I talked to people there who claimed that misappropriated Eurail passes were for sale cheap in Amsterdam, and I decided to check out that rumor. Walking in late morning to an autobahn onramp I saw a discouraging sight. There were already 9 groups of hitch-hikers strung out along the ramp. I followed hitcher etiquette, marching past all of them to put out my thumb as the 10ᵗʰ hitching party any driver would see. At the end of the day, tired and bored, only 3 drivers had stopped all day, and there were by then another 4 groups in line behind me. I gave up, walking wearily back to the huge, tented hostel for another night.

Miss Oh Five

Next morning I was up and out VERY early to the same ramp, which was dark and empty! I held out my "Netherlands" hitching sign, and after only a moment, a bright red 2-seat sportscar pulled over on the shoulder near me. The driver was an attractive young woman, stylishly dressed, who met my eye and beckoned me over. Carmen was driving to Den Haag to be interviewed by a writer, and she would take me there. Perfect! Those who have never hitch-hiked may be unaware that being picked up by a pretty gal in a sporty car was every guy's fantasy. Well, there I sat beside her as we accelerated up the ramp. Carmen's excellent English was displayed as we chatted during the drive northward. Carmen Thomas said she was a sportscaster on German television, actually the first female sports presenter! She agreed that the 'average' German sports fan just might recognize her. I told a few African vagabonding stories which seemed to be well received.

Before we left German territory a patrol car flashed its lights and sounded its siren. Carmen pulled over and took the registration out of her wallet. When the cop came up to the driver's window he flashed a grin MUCH too big for his small head and with apparent delight exclaimed "Fraulein Zero Fünf!" He had stopped us for an inoperable tail-light, but after providing him with two autographs, Carmen was not cited. As we drove onward I asked why the patrolman had called her "Fraulein Zero Fünf"? Looking slightly exasperated, Carmen admitted that her nickname was "Miss Oh Five" because on her very first televised appearance she had, for some unimaginable reason, called a little-known football team 'Schalke 1905' when the name was actually 'Schalke 1904'. Her slip of the tongue had thrilled her critics, and achieved near-legendary status. Carmen was content for fans to call her "Miss Oh 5", just as long as they continued to talk about her.

Reaching her destination of Den Haag, my new friend asked if I might stick around until after her interview, as she intended to treat me to dinner. That might have added an exclamation point to my 'perfect ride' fantasy, but I was too stuck on getting to my destination, so I thanked Carmen and apologetically turned away towards Amsterdam.

Carmen Thomas went on to have an interesting career. She worked for public radio, running a weekly traveling talk show for two decades. In 1990 Forbes named her one of the 100 most influential women in Germany. Carmen has since become a self-help author of some note.*

The Dutch

Arriving in Amsterdam, I was recruited to live on a canal barge which was being converted into a floating hostel. The 'skipper' was an American with a Dutch wife, and the remainder of the crew were some of the dregs of the populations of many third-world countries.

---

* https://en.wikipedia.org/wiki/Carmen_Thomas

Amsterdam Houseboat

The deal at the hostel/barge was that you could live there without paying if you agreed to do chores, or work towards the modifications, or would shill for new residents at the railway station. I was very successful at meeting one or two chosen trains each day before collecting backpackers and guiding them back to the barge.

Girls from New Jersey

One afternoon one of the crew called Raul appeared escorting three young, fresh American women. These gals were just off the plane from New Jersey, and quite physically attractive. All of us took note, and engaged one or another of them in conversation.

Soon, however, it became clear what a mistake Raul had made. The New Jersey girls were unquestionably 3 of the most BOR-ING people on earth, and now they were staying on our barge!

Pattie, with whom I was conversing, for some reason decided I needed to know everything about her neighbor's garage improvements, IN NAUSEATING DETAIL, how they had redesigned the layout, chosen the contractors, poured the cement, decided on curtain color, etc., etc., ad infinitum! After I had listened politely for WAY too long, the gals declared they were famished. They had heard there was a McDonald's somewhere in Amsterdam, and certainly didn't want to try any weird European food!! The skipper marked McDonalds' location on their tourist map, and off the three of them marched!! Night fell before they returned to find the barge all dark and silent. Actually four of us were hiding in the Skipper's cabin silently playing scrabble by the light of a single candle. The new Jersey girls stomped around the barge noisily calling out for someone to take them out to a club or a bar. We remained silent, desperately afraid our hideout would be discovered. Good fortune kept us secure.

Dodgy EuRail Pass

In Amsterdam, a small plaza outside the American Express office was the nexus for any vagabonding deal or scam, so I walked there. Asking folks whom I should contact to purchase a rail pass earned me no leads, and everyone seemed to be having trouble meeting my eyes. Finally decided that the cheap rail passes must have been imaginary.

Ten days later, after having my hand-cast removed, I went back to the American Express office and again asked one of the same folks I had previously queried. This time he immediately sold me a first-class Eurail pass good for unlimited travel for 3 months, and very inexpensive. He put my name on the pass, then heat-sealed it in a special plastic sheath with a small window through which it could be marked with the start date. I learned then, that on my earlier visit, folks were worried that my hand cast concealed recording equipment, and I had been judged a probable police informant.

Mexican Food?

As I climbed the inside stairs to American Express I saw a poster in a locked glass display frame which advertised Amsterdam's first Mexican Restaurant. It had been way too long since I had enjoyed Mexican food, so I noted down the address, and sought it out the next day. The restaurant had zero atmosphere, and the menu seemed rather expensive. Splurging, I ordered a burrito. What was handed to me across the counter was a tiny 4" diameter corn tortilla that they had just taken out of a can, wrapped around some brown chili sauce, the ends not even folded in so the sauce oozed out of both ends. It was one of the most disappointing things I had ever deliberately put in my mouth. After paying way too much, I attempted to coach the restaurant owner in how a 'burrito' should actually be assembled, so he could improve his act, but he dismissed my information with a sneer.

The next time I checked for mail at American Express I loitered half-way up the stairs by the Mexican Restaurant sign until nobody was in sight. I slipped a piece of paper into the top of the locked display case, and it fell perfectly across the bottom of the poster. My addition read:

Foul and Repulsive!

—a Californian

Somewhat remarkably, when I returned to Amsterdam 8 weeks later, my warning sign had not been removed and remained in place.

My railpass was no good in the United Kingdom, and once a start date was written on it, the 3-month timer would be ticking. My plan was to cross the channel and see everything in the United Kingdom and Ireland, then return to the continent and start the rail pass.

The VanRoelens

Satisfied with my stay on the Amsterdam barge, I hitch-hiked into Belgium, a town called Leuven. Geert Vanroelen had come to my high school as an exchange student and become part of my younger brother Matt's gang. He was a really free spirit, ready for any challenge, and a musician. Belgians might remember Geert as the leader of a noisy band called 'The Employees' which was briefly famous.

From Leuven I telephoned the best number I had for Geert, and connected with him. I hitched to the railway station where Geert's mom picked me up in her car and took me to the small town of Zoutleew, home to the Vanroelens. Geert arrived shortly and we built some bookshelves out of wooden fruit boxes. Geert's dad came home and immediately regaled me with the historical artifacts (broken smoking pipes and pottery) which they had excavated from their own lower garden. We picked apples for applesauce at Mr. Vanroelen's school, and I met a few younger sisters before dinner. The meal was very nice, and Mr. Vanroelen was in fine form talking about the modern fascists, and the movement in Flanders, and the Second World War, getting a bit out of hand and exaggerating liberally. I found it quite amazing that the entire family, even the little girls, spoke English well enough to carry on through the entire evening in that language, only because I couldn't speak Flemish.

Belgian Geert

Geert was studying Geography at the University in Brussels, so we proceeded there and spent a few days sleeping in the dormitories. With Geert's help I tried again to find Wehrmacht Hosenträger (German Army Battle Harness) for my brother Mark's collection, but without joy. Brussels has dozens of museums, and the most interesting few were visited. In an antique store I purchased a 300-year-old print of Zoutleew and gifted it to Geert's dad.

There was plenty of political turmoil in the air at the time, and a big protest march was planned by the Student/Worker alliance of Belgium. Geert invited me back in 12 weeks time as he wanted to show me how European demonstrations differed from their American counterparts.

To London

I headed for London, happy to use any ferry port to which I might score a ride. A package-tour-company troubleshooter picked me up in his Mercedes and drove me to downtown Calais. He returned to the car after a few minutes in his office, tossing a package of papers in my lap. His company had a tour group going back to London that same afternoon, and gave me a ticket across the straits of Dover with them, and then all the way to London on the train!! Some hours hence I tried hard to be inconspicuous as I moved up the narrow gangway to the ferry, head and shoulders taller than dozens of tiny English ladies in front of me and twenty more behind me.

I reached London that evening, two full days earlier than I had expected to. A big, run-down, excellent youth hostel near St. Pauls was discovered and checked in to.

London is probably the world's best city for museums. Several days were spent perusing the collections in the British Museum and The Science and Technology museum.

Never Say it to a Drunk

My fourth night in the 12-bed hostel dorm room, I was soundly asleep in one of the lower bunks. A young man loomed over me in the dark, grabbed my blankets, and began to tug on them urgently. I awakened to push his hand away. "Hey, Get lost, this is my bed!" I whispered. I could smell puke on him, so concluded that he was probably highly inebriated. He again tried to pull my blanket aside so he could climb in bed with me. "PISS OFF", I whispered, trying not to waken everyone else in the room.

Bunk Partner

The drunk straightened up unsteadily, looking down at me without speaking. He decided my suggestion was a good one. Pints of urine poured out of one pant leg onto the floor!! I immediately relocated my belongings out from the floor to the bunk at my feet to keep them dry. The drunk then walked all the way around the next set of bunks and climbed into bed under the covers of my poor snoozing neighbor, who did not awaken. I took a low-light photo of the very crowded bunk, and made a mental note to never again command a drunk to "Piss Off".

Stonehenge

After a week I shouldered my backpack and hitched to the west to visit Stonehenge. The Salisbury plain revealed its gently rolling terrain to me, and the famous standing stones appeared on the horizon. Arriving in the very early morning, I had the monument to myself for 45 minutes. I sat with my back against one of the huge vertical stones reading my guidebook. An elderly caretaker/guard came over to stand close-by, and as the fog slowly dissipated, we had a nice, quiet conversation. But the peace wasn't likely to last.

Approaching at high speed along the road, two tour busses were spotted, appearing and disappearing as the road climbed and dropped. The busses pulled into the sunken parking area and disgorged 80 American tourists. One of the first to reach the stones was a quick-moving woman wearing sparkling red-framed glasses. She clattered up to us, jammed her face within a foot of that of the silent caretaker and shrieked—"IS THIS WHERE THE SPACE-MEN LANDED?!?" My emotional harmony was thereby completely shattered, and I could no longer remain at Stonehenge, now over-run with quarter-wit, clueless Americans.

Undead Horror

Proceeding around Salisbury plain by foot and thumb, a number of other ancient sites were visited, including Avebury Circle, West Kennet Long Barrow, and Silbury Hill. The weather worsened in the evening, and standing hitching in the rain, I realized that I would not get a ride. Nobody desired a big, soaking wet, unknown guy in their vehicle! In other parts of the country I would have found a bridge and slept under it, but the Salisbury

Barrow Entrance

plains were too flat to offer such shelter. I thought again of West Kennet Long Barrow, a set of stone-age tombs at one end of a 200-yard-long mound of dirt. The barrow was less than a mile away, and I marched there as the light failed. Climbing over two styles and marching across three fields, I reached the unattended barrow tomb.

By then the wind was moaning across the plain, the raindrops stinging and moving almost horizontally. It was exceedingly dark. I could just barely tell the earth from the clouded sky. Once inside, my flashlight identified the driest of the 5 rock-built burial chambers before my plastic groundsheet and down sleeping bag were deployed. There inside nothing existed except the tiny pale green radium dots on the face of my cheap wristwatch. I put my boots next to my head, and the flashlight in the top of the boots, and settled in to sleep. But with the wind howling across the tomb entrance, as well as the memory that the bones of over 200 stone-age people had been buried in these small chambers, I couldn't claim that I was completely at ease. I pondered awhile about the Barrow Wights, legendary evil undead creatures supposed to inhabit the barrow tombs.

Just when I was Three-quarters asleep, the entire tomb was filled with LOUD terrifying sound!!

WHOOOSH—WHOOOSh—WHOOOsh—WHOoosh—Whooosh!

And SOMETHING grabbed my ankle through the down bag!!!!!!

My heart leapt to my throat, as I nearly soiled myself!! In total darkness I imagined that the Wight had taken hold of me to drag me away!!

Took me five of the LONGEST seconds of my life to realize that the big field birds had flown into the barrow to get out of the rain, and their long toes had alighted on me!!

I shouted that they should leave, but the invisible pheasants periodically flew in and out of the tomb all night, making restful sleep impossible

Leaving my pheasant room-mates behind in the morning, I hitched northward to visit the beautiful cathedral in York. Thumbing was pretty easy, and the fellowship every evening at British youth hostels was excellent.

On my way north, the well-preserved foundations of a section of Hadrian's Wall proved quite interesting to see. Roman Emperor Hadrian ordered the wall built all the way across Britain to defend against the northern tribes.

Hadrian's Wall

Caledonia

Continuing to Scotland, I enjoyed visiting various lochs and castles. A sedan rather crowded with ladies pulled over to have a close look at me. The bearded American guy driving ran down the window to ask if I could drive a stick shift. I agreed that this was within my skill set. Neal had rented the car, then picked up two young women, then a third, and made them all part of his crew. The gals greeted me from the other seats. The guy had done a good job of stacking the deck in his favor. But poor Neal had injured his ankle the day before, making it difficult for him to continue as the sole driver, and none of the gals could operate a manual transmission. I happily volunteered as driver, and joined the crew. Jody and Teresa were students from Oregon, Helen a masseuse from Indiana, and Neal was a techie from New England. Almost imme-

Jody, Teresa, Helen
Chick and Neal

diately I learned Jody's special talent. She could sing gorgeously EXACTLY like Joni Mitchell! Looked a bit like her as well.

Our posse traveled together all around Scotland for the next week. I did all of the driving, my first disconcerting experience of driving on the left. It surprised me how pleasant it was to have, for the first time in my vagabonding, solid control over where I would go, and where I would be at the end of the day. Meal preparation as a shared responsibility was also more agreeable than solo. I would have been glad to continue driving our team around for months, but it was not to be. Neal's return-flight date coincided with Jody and Teresa's plan to be somewhere else. Helen asked if we could travel together, which sounded fine. I wanted to visit Northern Ireland, even though the political situation was unsettled and things were dangerous there.

American Jews

My standard way of hitch-hiking had always been to walk rapidly in the direction of travel, turning around to walk backwards and hitch whenever a vehicle approached. No, I haven't tripped over things TOO many times while walking backwards. I soon discovered that Helen had very little physical stamina, so my hitch-hiking paradigm changed to sitting on our packs with destination sign displayed. We crossed the Irish Sea to Newcastle, then hitched to Belfast.

The Catholics and Protestants of Northern Ireland were not co-existing peacefully, and a few weeks earlier masked gunmen had stopped a night bus, separated the passengers into groups by professed religion, and then murdered (!) everyone in the less popular group!! The first thing all Northern Irish folks wanted to know was whether we were Catholic or Protestant. Since Helen was Jewish, we decided that we would both claim to be Jews for the duration of our time in the country. That worked pretty well, but we had to hear the same joke fifty times in the following weeks, each time pretending it was new to us. Fortunately it is a pretty good joke, as follows:

A Jewish American couple are driving along a lonely roadway at night when they come to a pair of flaming waste drums blocking the road. A masked gunman walks up to the driver's side of the car and motions with his revolver to the husband, who rolls down the window.

(Read with the broadest possible Irish accent)

"Now, ye'll be tellin' me, would ye be Cath-o-lics orrr Prrrrotestants?
"Actually" replies the driver, "we are American Jews."
"Ann tah be shoor, ye've goot NO luck tonoit. I'm the only Arrrab in Derrrry county!"

Northern Ireland

Playing cards at a youth hostel, the very best player, a northern Irishman, talked cogently and feelingly about both sides of the 'Irish problem', professing very aware and liberal views. But later in the evening we witnessed him loudly singing provocative Protestant fight songs!

We proceeded to visit legend-shrouded Giant's Causeway, on the very northern tip of the Island. This geologic wonder proved MUCH more interesting and photogenic than I expected. Being there one feels strongly that the Causeway could have been created by supernatural beings. We remained until the chilly wind drove us away to a hostel fireside.

Giant's Causeway

It proved very difficult to locate another little-known attraction. Only on foot, and with plenty of requests for directions did we find the Prehistoric Fortified Island of Lough na Crainach. It sat offshore in a small lake, and it was necessary to deal with a Large, territorial Bull in order to reach the shore. They say that the approach path sits under 8" of water, and has several unannounced right angle turns to cause sneaky marauders to miss the path, fall in the water, and thereby warn the stone-age defenders. Nobody else visited while we lingered at Lough na Crainach, and I've never met another person who actually has visited the site.

Giant's Causeway

In Londonderry County a large, imposing Tudor/Gothic mansion had been converted into a youth hostel. However, there really were no backpackers in that area and this season. Helen and I checked in and had the unusual experience of booking the entire Learnmount Castle for only $2 per night.

Another unappealing local past-time was throwing bombs into government facilities. To prevent this, one saw occasional HIGH chain-link fences surrounding police stations and public buildings.

Fortified Island Lough na Crainach

Anti-Thrown-Bomb Screen

Finding and recording genuine folk music was something that Helen loved to do. In both Derry and Omagh she deployed her simple recording equipment to capture impromptu musical performances which tended to suddenly blossom anywhere in Northern Ireland where people sat to talk and drink.

Republic of Ireland

Helen had a friend named Cathy in Galway whom she wanted to visit so we crossed the border into Ireland proper and traveled southward for two days. Cathy was in town and put us up for the night in her housemates' room. The next morning I parted from Helen, now safely in Cathy's orbit, and hitch-hiked easily 200 km to Blarney castle, which had JUST closed for the evening. Cork's big youth hostel wasn't that far away, so I crashed there. I visited Blarney castle and allowed the local boys to support me as I leaned way out under the battlements to kiss the famous stone. Back at the hostel I was astonished to find that Helen had followed me to Cork. Previously professing no interest in me, she now timidly invited affection.

I headed out solo again in the morning, with Dublin as my goal. Wales was beckoning me, so I headed for the ferry landing which would carry me there.

I stopped at a chemist's shop and stood in line with a half-dozen other customers. When my turn brought me up to the counter I asked the nice, grey-haired shop lady to sell me condoms. All chat in the line behind me ceased immediately.

She looked at me with compassion, and motioned me to follow her down to the end of the counter, where she could move closer to me and whisper in my ear. "A very Catholic country is Ireland. Not only is it against the law for me to sell those, but it is illegal for you to ask for them." I apologized, and thanked her for handling my crime with kindness and delicacy.

Looking into the Face of god

Hitch-hiking around Wales, I mostly visited ancient monuments.

I do highly recommend Caerphilly as the quintessential storybook castle. It has a wide moat, curtain walls, round towers, a picturesque gatehouse, and a substantial keep. Also available there are plenty of colorful legends. If you can see only a single Castle in Great Britain, make it Caerphilly.

I headed south along a minor road which wandered through gently rolling countryside. Only one lane in each direction, then ditches on both sides of the road, and waist-high dry-stone walls backing the ditches around each orchard. In late afternoon I found myself marching generally southwest. My paradigm for hitching is to march purposefully in the direction of travel, spinning around to display my destination sign whenever a vehicle approached, and continuing to walk backwards. The weather was good, no rain in the forecast, my equipment was in good repair, and I was satisfied, hoping to find somewhere comfortable to sleep. I heard a small engine approaching and spun around to thumb a tiny Morris Minor carrying three large Welsh lads. They all gave me a really 'hard' look as they zoomed up the hill. The Morris stopped at the top of the long hill, and I could see three arms out of three windows motioning for me to come on up for a ride, so I ran quite a distance uphill, realizing that they hadn't stopped for me at the bottom so as not to lose their momentum. Made sense since their engine was small in proportion to the load it was hauling.

When I nearly reached the crest I could see the large young Welshman in the back seat beckoning me from behind the rear window. Both front windows displayed brawny arms waving to me to "come on!" The face I could see changed to a smirk as the Morris slowly began to move, pulling away. All 3 arms now gave me the British two-fingered "Screw You!" gesture. Completely out of energy, I slowed down, defeated and angry. Those guys really had no reason to deceive me in that way. Purely to get some of the frustration out of my system, I scooped up a smooth golf-ball sized half-cobble, and pitched it with all my strength up at a 45 degree angle above the rapidly moving Morris. I had no real intent of hitting it, as it was far by now, and nobody can throw accurately wearing a heavy backpack.

The sun had nearly set to the right of the road as I watched, my chest still heaving. But that projectile arced unerringly, long and accurate, down to make contact with the upper right corner of the car's rear window. It was too far for me to hear any impact, but I saw two tiny flashes of reflection from glass shards as they caught the fading sunlight! I had broken the Morris Minor's rear window!!! I stood gawking, totally surprised and shocked. The Morris braked, turned onto the left shoulder, and braked again to a halt. A few seconds later it started to reverse up the hill towards me!

My entire being was immediately illuminated with the **most powerful blast of fierce JOY** I've ever known! Every fiber of me was SO incandescently happy that my knees nearly folded! And I knew at that moment I was looking into the face of god. It was NOT, however, our kind, forgiving, merciful Judeo-Christian God, but rather the Roman deity Mars, god of Bloody War!! All of my consciousness focused on a single wonderful concept—

"They are Coming Back!
—I get to Kill Them All!!"

Swooning with unalloyed Joy I reached over my shoulder to seize the Maasai War Club strapped to my backpack. Both hands gripped it tightly as the vehicle moved closer. At just that instant a Lorry came over the hill from behind me, spotted the Morris in its path, and SLAMMED both the brakes and the horn! Screeching tires and dust and confusion masked my view of the target. This interruption gave me the crucial 10 seconds I needed to re-engage my logic circuits and realize that I was going to LOSE that fight, and even if by some amazing chance I managed to win, I would be spending time in Prison for murder! So I jumped the roadside ditch, then the orchard wall, and moved 100 yards into the apple grove before concealing myself behind the trunk of an ancient tree!!

My Welsh opponents disentangled themselves from the Lorry and climbed out of the car, furious and belligerent. They marched up and down the nearby road for twenty minutes, slandering me using very rude names, challenging my cowardly self to reappear and face their wrath. They finally grew hoarse and drove away. I waited in hiding a full hour expecting them to circle back around, but it didn't happen. Gambling that a daring move might succeed, I hitched a ride in the same direction, watching other cars very carefully in case the bullies had disguised themselves by changing vehicles. I was lucky, or they were lazy, because I was never called to account for my low-probability cobble toss. I really hope those jerks didn't take out their frustration on the next longhaired hitch-hiker they encountered.

Sights of England

From Wales I returned to England, still visiting ancient monuments. Maiden Castle with its huge Iron-Ave scarps and ditches impressed me greatly.

I spent most of a day digging ammonite fossils out of the chalky cliffs at Lyme Regis on the Jurassic south coast.

By that date the promise of mail waiting for me at American Express in Amsterdam lured me back across the channel. This time I paid my own way. The dodgy rail pass was initialized, and I quickly learned some of the many ways that an unlimited first class pass could be used and abused.

Useful Rail Pass

When sleeping on the upholstered bench in a first class carriage, I tended to wrap my head up in my Palestinian black and white checked head cloth, which I called my 'Al Fatah Towel.' Passengers peering into the carriage would likely believe a middle-eastern gentleman was snoozing within, and their Xenophobia often caused them to move on to sit in a different carriage, making more room for me to sleep comfortably. Also, in cases where I hadn't secured lodging, it was easy to find and board a train heading somewhere remote, and sleep all the way there, returning asleep in the early hours of the morning after a reasonably comfortable, free night's lodging.

Lands of the Vikings

The railpass carried me north to have a look around the Scandinavian countries. From Amsterdam I arrived in Stockholm about 1 am. By the time I climbed up to street level from the underground station, all the other passengers had already departed. At the top of a flight of 20 stairs stood an unusually attractive Swedish woman. She was one of those gals, (guys will know what I mean when I say this) who when you first spot her, no matter how far away, your butt muscles tighten up just a bit. This vision was smiling big at me, and making full eye contact. When I got close to her she asked me something, a long sentence in musical Swedish. I apologized in English for not understanding Swedish. She changed her approach and just asked "Hash??" She was meeting the express from Amsterdam in hopes that some guy would share his stash with her. At that moment I really regretted that I hadn't brought any Hash with me. Then again, it was not impossible that the lovely gal was working with the Police.

I nosed around Sweden, Denmark, and Norway. Vagabonding in the Scandinavian countries was relatively expensive when compared to other parts of the world, and I was determined to stretch my traveling money as much as reasonably possible.

I remember enjoying the Wasa dockyard, where the sunken Swedish flagship had been raised and was being refurbished. In Oslo, the Kon Tiki museum drew my attention. As a child I had avidly read all of Thor Heyerdahl's books.

Finland Imbalance

In another Scandinavian note, it was said that in Finland, for some unknown reason, the proportion of new births was out of balance. Over the remainder of Europe, 48 male babies survived infancy for every 52 girl babies. In Finland it was said to be 3 boys for every 4 girls, thereby resulting in very large numbers of Finnish lasses who would not be able to find a corresponding Finnish man. I couldn't really believe these startling statistics until they were confirmed in an interesting way. I met a Dutchman on the train who said he had a Finnish wife, and that it was generally known in Holland that if you had trouble finding a girlfriend, you should simply find a job in Finland, and shortly that problem would be solved. Jens and his wife belonged to a group exclusively for Dutch/Finnish couples, and of the 800+ member couples, only 3 were Finnish guys and Dutch gals!!! This amazing circumstantial evidence notwithstanding, my web research in 2023 indicates that the Finnish Male/Female Birth Rate was only an old wives tale, and wasn't based in fact.

Paris and Beyond

I used my spiffy new rail pass to carry me to Paris for the very first time. I had been a bit worried about travel in France because some folks said the French could be very brusque and rude to tourists who were unable to speak French. I had studied French in high school, and could speak and understand it after a fashion, but was by no means fluent. In the huge underground railway station I collected information on how to find the main, central French Tourist office, which was on the Champs Elysees. Two backpacker girls accosted me in a language I didn't recognize. Celia and Jill were South Africans and had tried speaking Afrikaans to me before switching to English. Each of them were engaged to be married, and were having their European fling before going home for the weddings. They too sought the central Tourist Office, but couldn't get any directions. They realized that I could speak apparently understandable French, and attached themselves to me for the next few days.

I figured out how to navigate the Metro and we rode it to the Champs Elysees. We walked along that lovely boulevard to the main tourist office, and I asked our questions in quiet French. Wow, the women behind the counter just about cut me dead with their cold, detached, monosyllabic replies. They looked right through me rather than acknowledge my presence. I finally assembled the information we needed, but it was so difficult it seemed like sucking golf balls through a garden hose. I knew then that communicating would be very difficult in France.

However, that bad experience speaking with the women who are PAID TO HELP TOURISTS was by far the worst such experience I ever had in France. Everyone else in the country was very friendly and kind to me, listening carefully as I butchered their language, and speaking slowly and clearly to me in return. As night was falling we rode the Metro to two different youth hostels to find both completely full. Then we discovered a small guest house room with 3 beds, much nicer than the hostels, and only half the price if split 3 ways. That evening Jill and Celia taught me about the exciting South African sport of 'Couch Rugby', though only in the abstract, and without any demonstrations.

My War Grave

I had another pilgrimage on my mental list. In 1945 my father Walt was really crushed by the loss of his much-loved oldest brother in Holland late in the 2nd World War. I had been named Charles in honor of Uncle Chuck, and I carried the address and telephone number of a Dutch gal named Mia who had nursed

My name on the Gravestone

Chuck through a previous war injury, and had been maintaining his military grave ever since. Rails carried me easily to Maastricht and the huge American military cemetery there. The guy on duty at the cemetery desk helped me find my namesake's grave marker on a map, and I hiked there to stand awhile in silent contemplation. It was strange to see my own name carved into the white marble cross.

I tried telephoning Mia, but never managed to reach her, though I left voice messages. Purchasing a nice winter-flowering yellow-blossomed plant, I found my way to Mia's modest flat and left that small gift along with a letter thanking her for her kindness over the years.

Back to Amsterdam I rode, to celebrate Thanksgiving with two dozen other American expats on the hostel barge. My folks sent me money to telephone home on my 26th birthday. International communications were much more difficult in those days and it wasn't easy to set the call up ahead of time. We had a decent connection, though a bit 'scratchy'. It was really nice to hear all the home crowd's voices after 11 months on the road.

Worker/Student Alliance in Belgium

Passing back and forth through Brussels, Geert's dorm floor was frequently my bed. He was trying to tame a young feral cat living around the dorms. I suggested we use catnip as a lure for the kitty. I was surprised to learn that Europeans in general have never heard of catnip. Geert didn't believe what I told him about the effects of the herb until he saw it demonstrated. I did manage to purchase a handful of catnip at the local spice market, although it was a pretty stale sample. We mixed it with the feral kitty's food, and soon were laughing hard at the 'inebriated' behavior of the young feline. She allowed herself to be captured and wrapped up tightly in a kitchen towel, so that Geert could finally hug and kiss her as much as he wanted to.

The Belgian government had made some budget decisions which were not popular with the university students. A huge sum was earmarked to purchase fighter jets from the USA, while simultaneously removing funding from the university to the point where they were forced to actually close down Geert's Geography department. He would still be able to receive a Geography degree, but future students would not have that option.

A big demonstration was planned by the Belgian Worker/Student Alliance. Papers were filed with the city, defining exactly the route the march would follow. If that route came too near the central heart of Brussels, then the demonstration march would not be approved. Only if the route confined itself to the poorer suburbs of the city would approval be granted. So the compromise, as in previous years, was that a route which would not inconvenience very many citizens was approved, but the demonstrators all understood that at some point the march would 'go rogue' and make its way into the central district, snarling traffic and becoming as unavoidable and obnoxious as possible.

Geert, his student buddies and I began as one small contingent of the demonstration march, as it formed up early in the morning out in a remote suburb. Already the police presence was heavy, but weather cooperated, chilly and clear. We happily marched, continuously voicing a pleasant-tuned chant—"Arbeiter Studenten Een Vroont". (Workers and Students, One Front) The various marching contingents each included a few guys incongruously carrying shopping bags, and the protest signs carried by some were mounted on suspiciously thick, heavy sticks.

Up at the faraway front of the march we could see a 20 foot long painted banner supported by a 20 foot high pole on either end. The march organizers carried walkie-talkies, and used them to pass messages up and down the march column.

Geert had schooled me on march protocol. In his shopping bag was a heavy woolen muffler to protect him from tear gas, thick padded motorcycle gloves, and one of his souvenirs from California, a Los Angeles Rams football helmet, big yellow curling horns painted on each side, complete with protective face cage. When the demonstration inevitably 'went rogue' he would don his protective gear.

As we moved along the approved route the police riot units, with helmets, sticks, and transparent shields, could be occasionally seen moving along parallel routes keeping up with the demonstrators. After maybe an hour and a half walking, a VERY different chant swept back along the column from those at the head of the march. This chant wasn't a pleasant tune at all, it was aggressive, faster, and somehow menacing. Geert's translation of this new chant was "We have had fun so far, but now it is going to get HOT!" I noticed the shopping bags passing us up, hurrying to the head of the march. Geert waved for me to run forward with him. I hesitated. "Geert, do we really want to directly challenge the cops?" "Come on", he replied, "the police don't want to meet the 'sharp end' hard core protestors, they will concentrate on beating up and arresting the softest, most passive and helpless targets!—Up at the front with all the helmets and gas masks is the SAFEST place for us to be!"

We reached the long banner to find that the heavy long poles were being broken into approximately 3 foot long lengths and handed out to demonstrators eager to receive them. Geert put on his Rams helmet and gloves, and wrapped the muffler around his neck. We passed a nondescript guy on the sidewalk using a walkie-talkie who was promptly hit with several thrown eggs as a police informant. The cross streets now were uniformly blocked off solidly by wire entanglements and/or double ranks of riot police. A mounted police unit could be seen maneuvering ahead, and police cars and sirens were in evidence in every direction. It definitely was 'getting HOT'.

Going Rogue

Without warning, the entire front contingent of the march, including perhaps 70 helmeted and gas masked miscreants, headed off to the right, sprinting up a cross street which the police had failed to solidly block. Two police cars pulled quickly across the road, but the flood of demonstrators went RIGHT over and around them, stomping on the hoods and roofs, moving as quickly as possible!! We tucked ourselves right up against the helmets and motorcycle gloves, running to keep up with the crowd. Behind us the 'softer' parts of the demonstrator crowd were being drawn along. There were plenty of police assets on either side of our path, preparing something by getting into position.

The Belgian hard-asses thundered across yet one more cross street, and I could see a column of riot police running at right angles to our direction to cut us off. They passed just behind me, chopping the demonstrator's column off at the head. Though I couldn't see it, we found out afterward that two additional columns of police had snipped the march neatly into four pieces. They had been only 10 seconds too late to also capture us at the very head. We stood, confused, lungs heaving, as the realization sank in that there were no obstacles directly ahead of us. Then, with joyful cries, the uncorralled 120 marchers took off again running towards the center of Brussels!!

Law Enforcement Central

Unexpectedly, we popped out of the street which had restricted our view into the central vista of Brussels, a ½ mile diameter area including two large parking lots and criss-crossed by numerous roads and elevated ramps! We all took a big breath! On the far side of the view were the central library and the main Railway Station, as well as the Belgian Parliament building. Crowds of Belgian civilians moved about on their normal routines. Then the details swam into focus. I could see 500 riot armed police in twenty well-ordered units, plus 40 police squad cars and 20 busses. Halfway up the opposite slope squatted two ugly Police Armored Cars, each mounted with two water-cannons. To the right a group of 30 mounted police cantered towards the center of the view. The forbidden hub of Brussels was **Law Enforcement Central!**

Just to our front two empty police busses flew from right to left on a connecting ramp. The drivers hunkered down and turned their faces away as a dozen large, heavy half-bricks, carried for just such an opportunity, smashed through windows on our side of the busses!! Geert seemed fine with this development, but I realized that, after this unprovoked violence on the part of us demonstrators, anything the forces of order might do to us would be justified. The padded boxing gloves were off! It would be a bare-knuckle fight from here onward.

Apparently a decision was made, and the remaining small cadre of unconstrained protestors moved forward once more, right into the teeth of the government defenses. The mounted police unit dressed its line in front of us, awaiting a command. We protestors slowed down and stopped, standing in the street, tired out, our momentum spent, finally uncertain of the next move.

This decision was taken out of our hands as the line of horsed cops came forward at the walk, then accelerated to a trot. Each officer carried a ½" thick flexible metal-bound baton four feet long. Grinning behind their face shields they swung the batons in slow vertical circles. These policemen had done this before and they REALLY enjoyed it!!

As the equestrians trotted nearer, the protesting crowd simply vaporized. Nobody was willing to face the accelerating horse-police charge, and it was everyone for himself!! Geert led me laterally into one of the parking lots. He had worked there a year previously, and knew it was private property onto which the gendarmes could not legally pursue a demonstrator. Geert's Rams helmet disappeared into a previously identified hiding place, along with the shopping bag. We moved part way up a very long stairway which led up the slope towards the Parliament building and watched the various police contingents. After a moment of heated discussion at the entrance gate of the parking lot, the police suddenly swarmed inside. They really wanted to arrest the half-dozen helmeted demonstrators remaining there, and legal niceties were not about to deter them. Most of the remaining hard-asses sprinted into the tunnels leading below the library and parliament buildings. Two obvious motorcycle helmets climbed the stairs past us, with 4 police slowly following at some distance. We felt pretty secure since there were five different roads leading away from the top of our stairs, so we dawdled.

Mistake, a second previously-unseen horse police unit appeared at the canter, sealing off all of the routes by which we might retreat!! They had VERY neatly trapped us. So—we copped out. As the foot police approached near, Geert and I mixed ourselves in with some of the hundreds of innocent citizens. We sat down on a low wall and began pointing things out to one another, commenting loudly in English as though we were clueless American tourists rather than actionable criminals. The climbing cops went right past us without even an interested glance!! We were safe, and slowly, painstakingly worked our way through the completely messed up and snarled traffic back to the University.

The demonstration had definitely succeeded in its aim of bringing the students' grievances to the notice of the media and the man in the street. Public transport was still knocked out at 8 pm, and the newspapers and programs the following day were full of little else. I was secretly glad to add the experience of being on the receiving end of a horse cavalry charge to my life-resume.

On the Loose in Europe

At this stage of my journey I used the rail-pass to crisscross back and forth across Europe, centering on France, but going as far as Pompeii in Italy, Gibraltar in the far south of Spain, Portugal,

Gibraltar
From
Spain

Switzerland, and Amsterdam, sometimes in company with other backpackers I had encountered. Such a list of "Then I went, then I saw" would rapidly grow boring and confusing, so I'll simply tell the stories which stand out in my memory without trying to string them together into a coherent sequential travelogue. After the rail pass expires, I will again write sequentially.

The ancient Bayeux tapestry and lovely Mont St. Michel on the French coast had always interested me, and both were visited. A train south carried me to near the very impressive, still standing Roman aqueduct at Pont du Gard.

Christmas was spent in a small mountain village called Bardou. The road leading into the area was only a glorified footpath in 1975/76. None of the stone-built houses had electricity or running water. The region was a huge forest of chestnut trees which were no longer harvested. The ruins of Bardou had been purchased by a German guy and his American wife, who were slowly rebuilding and renovating the 30 or so ruined stone houses. It was known that if you were willing to work on the renovations, one could live in Bardou nearly for free. When I arrived the Christmas feast planning was well along so I contributed mostly money to secure my seat at one of the tables. It was discovered that I could deliver a really good foot massage, and the men of Bardou were unsettled by the enthusiasm with which their various ladies lined up along a long bench so that I would minister to their tired feet in turn.

Spain was welcoming and cheap for backpackers at the time. Madrid, Barcelona, Toledo, and Valencia all have plenty of fascinating historical attractions. Riding to a city called Mérida I could see a fortress perched on a hilltop some distance out of town. I walked there and up through the ruined fortress gate, into a very macabre scene. Inside the curtain wall of the fortress was a large cemetery last used in the 1890s. Every grave and/or mausoleum inside had been broken open and the remains were scattered. Gave me the shivers, I'll tell you. Back in town I used my 30 words of Spanish to try to learn what had occurred there, and who might have desecrated all those graves, but nobody appeared to know that there was even a cemetery on that hill.

Merida Desecrated Graveyard

I aimed my rail pass at Portugal, but my timing was really bad. At the time the situation in Angola, a Portuguese colonial outpost in Africa, was unraveling, with most of the ethnically European Angolans fleeing to Lisbon. Every single bed in Lisbon was booked, with waiting lists. Every park or open space or sidewalk in Lisbon was covered with new tent-slums, leaving not even enough room for me to hide and nap. I rode the train back out of Lisbon that same night late, returning to Spain.

I rode the rails through the beautiful Swiss landscapes, but only spent one night in Bern due to the high cost of vagabonding there. Food and lodging in Switzerland were twice as expensive as in France.

Really enjoyed re-visiting Pompeii to show it so some new friends. Two consecutive travel-mates called themselves "Jackie" and each was headed to Pompeii when I encountered them. The rail pass made it nearly free to accompany each of them to southern Italy for another and then one more look around Pompeii.

Austrians Follow the Rules

When my 90-day rail pass was about to expire, I headed for Eastern Europe. The youth hostel I had used when I previously visited Vienna was in Esterhazy Park, and I worked out how to get there by switching on and off of various busses. There were two Italian long-distance busses parked outside the hostel, visiting Vienna for some sort of cheerleader competition. It was snowing rather hard when I tried to check in, but Helmut, the guy behind the desk in the large, warm, clean lobby told me the hostel was full, and I couldn't stay. I explained that I had nowhere else to go, but he was unimpressed. When asked if I might just sleep on one of the eight padded benches in the lobby, and check in the following morning, Helmut showed no spark of compassion.

So I went out into the snowstorm and circled around the hostel into the uphill part of the park. I crawled into the dark, snow-free space under a substantial evergreen tree, set up my tent, and prepared to sleep. I locked eyes with a warmly-clothed Austrian couple walking their dog, who strolled downhill on the path past my hiding place. Shortly the Hostel desk guy appeared, so angry that his fists were shaking!! Helmut shouted that I was to leave IMMEDIATELY and never return!! The rule-following Austrian couple had realized that dangerous criminals such as I should be reported to the authorities.

I packed up everything and walked down towards the road in the falling snow. The hostel guy accompanied me, assuring that I would not again misbehave. Then I noticed something strange. The top 4 floors of the 6-story hostel building were all completely dark and silent. Helmut controlled over 300 warm, empty beds in the upper floors which he wouldn't offer to me, and was still jealous of six feet of frozen ground out back! I do not think I will ever understand the Austrians, and might be lucky if I never do.

Out on the road I walked only a half-mile before I found a construction site which wasn't secured completely. The night there sleeping on frozen new concrete wasn't very restful, but it kept the snow off my face.

Land of the Magyars

I crossed the border into Hungary, ending the day in Budapest. The hostels were all either closed or full, but folks found me a very cheap bed in the gun chambers of the massive Citadella fortress. All of the walls were more than six feet thick, and rooms and galleries had domed roofs.

The Hungarians had an annoying rule which forced me to exchange a minimum amount of money, at RIPOFF government official rate, in order to enter the country. This was substantially more than I would spend in my three days in Hungary, so I sought out ways to use up my forints. I found a dentist who carefully cleaned and checked my teeth, and also bought two HUGE Hungarian salamis which I carried with me to Romania and ate at my leisure. My cholera inoculation, once I found the proper office, was delivered gratis. To burn my last few forints I purchased an entire kilo of excellent Swiss cheese.

Sitting in the wan sunlight in front of the Hungarian Communist Party Headquarters I witnessed a very strange method of clearing snow from the large paved plaza outside. Five women each had a conveyance like a trash can on wheels, and they shoveled in snow from the plaza until the cans were ⅓rd full. They then wheeled the cans over to stand in line with their co-workers until it came their turn to dump the little pile of snow beside an open manhole. A sixth gal's job was to shovel the snow piles down through the manhole. It was unbelievably inefficient, but apparently good enough in a communist country.

Land of the Romani

I hitch hiked south to the border of Romania. There the uniformed, beribboned soldiers at the border post asked me what my frisbee was. I explained it to them, then moved back a few steps, and threw it to one guy, who, eyes wide, caught it and grinned. Soon six of them stood around a piece of parking lot playing frisbee gleefully. A soldier with a fancier uniform stalked out of the office building. **Wham, the game was Over!** All my new friends stomped to rigid attention and walked, stiff legged, back to their stations.

My new border-guard buddies had a problem with a pair of Arab brothers and asked for my assistance. The Arabs were taking their used Mercedes home to Syria, but spoke only Arabic and English, and neither had the necessary international driver's license. I interceded in the communications, translating the guard's French into English, until finally the unfortunate Arabs understood the crux of their dilemma.

Bucharest was reached that afternoon by thumb. But I had blown the timing. It was Sunday, so everything was closed. I found a bench at a large central city park and read my books. A nice, well-dressed middle-aged man sat with me, introducing himself at a teacher of English. We had a fascinating conversation, with me hearing astonishing truths about his communist overlords, dominated by the Russians, while he used me to fill in small gaps in his own understanding of life in the west. When it was time to part, he apologized abjectly for not inviting me home with him, because, as he said, "The Police would come."

That evening I met a guy named Sylviu who offered to show me around the military museum in the morning. We rode trams and more trams, there is no way I would have found the place without help. The museum exhibits were very good, and most of the signs had English translations.

I offered to treat for lunch so we walked to a restaurant known to Sylviu. However, this restaurant was unexpectedly fancy, and Sylviu ordered lots more than I wanted for both of us. Liver, sausage, salad, mineral water, funny cheesy paste, and LOTS of unexplained hidden charges appeared on the invoice. The total was 64 lei, but I only had 50 lei to my name, and they wouldn't accept French Francs, the only other cash money I happened to carry. A compromise was worked out, but I departed from Sylviu feeling sad that I had been deliberately manipulated into paying for the most pointlessly expensive mediocre meal I suffered in my entire journey.

Land of the Bulgars

At the border crossing to Bulgaria the transit visa fee was very expensive, over three days traveling budget, and the exchange rate was correspondingly lousy. Powdery freak snow covered the ground, Making every vista picturesque. I stayed on the main road to Turkey.

At the border I walked through a truck park and fell in with Alec, a Scottish truck driver taking a trailer full of airplane parts directly through to Iran!! He had an empty bunk in the cab of his big, modern truck and kindly offered it to me. I really had no intention of missing all the interesting places in Turkey and the Middle East, so I politely declined, asking if he might carry me only to Istanbul, a day and a half ahead.

Winter grips Bulgaria

On the drive, Alec taught me a lot about the perils of international trucking. His windshield and windows were defended with particularly heavy chain-link-fence material supported by steel frames. He carried a whole case of cans of unspecified food which he had bought at home at a steep discount for cans without labels. Two or three of these he would throw out of the windows before known danger points in the hopes that the bandits known to be hiding above the road would refrain from rolling big rocks down onto his rig as he passed. Alec was part of a convoy of nine trucks such as his own, and his place in the column was seventh truck. No personal defense weapons were carried, because they would risk stiff prison sentences if discovered. These drivers were very highly compensated for their time, and for the dangers they faced.

British Long-Distance Truckers

The Sublime Porte

Alec dropped me off outside the capital of Turkey and I caught an inexpensive bus to very near the center of backpacker Istanbul, Yenner's Café, with Pudding Shops around the corner. I drank tea there and spent awhile reading his crazy books. Anybody could write whatever they chose in Yenner's blank journals. Most of it is, naturally, crap, with very occasional gems.

"Live like you lose it tomorrow—Learn like you live it forever!"

I told a few stories from Africa. Yenner seemed to take a liking to me, awarding me a glass of arak and an ovation.

From that moment on, Istanbul has remained one of my favorite cities on earth. The Turks were generally friendly and mostly trust-worthy. I peered across the Bosphorus strait for my first glimpse of Asia. The Topkapi Palace ("Tope-CAH-pee") and museum hold some of the most interesting items around, including a tooth, swords, bows, and hair of the prophet Mohammed himself!! The ancient Theodosian defensive walls may be the strongest ever designed, and are in surprisingly good repair. Istanbul's covered souk (Grand Bazaar) is enormous, and perfectly impossible to nav-

Streetcorner Graveyard

igate upon first visit. The immense Blue Mosque is gaspingly beautiful. The many, many layers of history covered up by the modern city are fascinating. Hagia Sophia, originally the gigantic home cathedral of the Eastern Orthodox religion, was converted into a mosque by conquering Sultan Mehmed II, then more recently into a museum. If you have never strolled around Istanbul, you really should consider putting it on your list.

On a tip I walked to the military museum on Friday to hear the Janissary Band perform. They wore 1700s period costumes and played many almost-familiar instruments. The music was really exhilarating, with loud drums, chanting, and strange eastern beats mixed with western military rhythms. I was all wound tight after listening to the inspiring music, eager to go out and slay any number of the infidel!!

Mideast Maneuvers

Six nights in Istanbul satisfied me, and soon I took a cheap bus across the strait to Asia and southward along the coast to the archaeological site of Troy. The weather was blustery and cold as I walked through the confusingly-signposted excavations. Other than myself, only 3 Germans in a badly-bashed-in BMW visited that day.

Hitched a ride to Izmir. It was very cold and stormy, with sleet and slush predominating from the gray weather. I tried to find inexpensive lodging for the night, but it wasn't easy. Finally a guest house halfway up the hill showed me a tiny room, only 4 feet wide and 6 long, built under a stairway.

In the common room I opened my Spanish 'flick knife' with its spring-loaded blade, and it caused quite a stir! Every man in the room was determined that I should sell it to him, and they tried to bully me into relinquishing the knife. Apparently having a flick-knife would immediately increase the masculine image of the local men.

Decision point

My miniature room was warm and cozy enough, but I spent the evening questioning whether I really wanted to continue all across Asia and the rest of the planet before once again seeing my friends and family in California. I was homesick, I guess, but decided that if I gave up and went home now, I would always

Pamukkale Formations

regret it, and there was a distinct risk that I might never get myself loose again.

In the morning the weather was crystal clear and crisp, with the gleaming blue sea visible down the valley as I marched down the hill to the main road. The market was awakening, the spices showed their vivid colors and exotic fragrances, and it was clear that I had made the correct decision by forging onward.

I walked through a roadside bus station on my way south out of town. The boys running the place sat me down and fed me good hot tea, and wanted to sell me a bus ticket. I told them a little bit about the joys of 'autostopping' (the local name for hitch-hiking in English). They then GAVE me a bus ticket, gratis all the way to my next destination of Denizli. The amazing Travertine Terraces of Pamukkale ("pum-oo-KAH-lay") were visited the same late afternoon. Pamukkale has been a health resort continuously for 2500 years, and modern tourists and spa-guests jammed all of the hot spring facilities which closely surrounded the photogenic terraces.

Canine Marauder

I hitch-hiked towards Antalya on the southern coast. Tramping along the road all alone, an enormous dog, trained to kill wolves and protect the local flocks, decided that my lumpy backpacker silhouette presented a threat to his sheep, and rushed down the hill towards me. That should not have been a problem, as I had spent a summer reading electric meters in Los Angeles, and therefore was not the least bit afraid of dogs, having met many thousands on their home territories. Roaring fiercely and waving my arms over my head, I moved towards the dog. That would, I knew, turn away 19 dogs out of 20. He never missed a stride. I pretended to throw something heavy at the rapidly approaching dog. That would turn away 99 out of 100 dogs. He accelerated, barking and snarling. This was that 100th dog! I had wasted all of my prep time, and now he was HERE!!

The fierce mutt desired nothing more than to tear off my leg, and was quite capable of doing so, snapping and snarling as we spun around together. I barely deflected his teeth with my extended left foot while hurrying to free my Maasai warclub attached to the backpack!!

Finally armed and balanced, I struck at my canine assailant, missing the head blow, only hitting him glancingly on the shoulder! The big wolf-killing dog gave a shrill "YIPE" and retreated 20 feet, still barking furiously. Surprisingly, I had not yet been bitten. A few minutes of noisy standoff later two shepherds walked languidly down the slope to restrain their helpmate. They had not witnessed him trying to dismember me. I was all blasted full of adrenalin, and had trouble relaxing enough to sleep that night.

Later that same evening I accidentally left my warclub on the truck which had carried me to Antalya. Pfui, but at least it had been available to deflect the giant wolf-killing dog.

Antalya

Atrocity Stories

In Antalya that evening a number of English-speaking Turks in the tea-shop told me the atrocity story of how Greek soldiers on Cyprus had killed pregnant Turkish women, and paraded around with the babies on their bayonets. They did NOT want to hear that I had listened to exactly that same tale in Greece, except there it was Turkish soldiers who were the culprits. I explained that I didn't believe either story, and neither should they. Both hate propaganda machines were promulgating the same lies to de-humanize their opponents, and it was our job, as good citizens and human beings, to identify and disregard their lies!!

Four lazy days were happily spent on the lovely beach at Alanya. After the frozen terrain farther north, the calm, sunny days seemed like a real Idyll.

Sites in Turkey

Recent archaeological discoveries at a Turkish site claimed that Catal Huyuk (chah-tahl-hoo-YEWK") was this planet's first settled town. The inland location was obscure to the local people. There were no signs, and the farm track which led there wasn't marked. A tractor coming along the lane stopped and allowed me to sit on one of the fenders, carrying me for the last 4 km. When I arrived, there was nothing to indicate that I had found my destination, only a corrugated iron building with a single blasé guard who arose from his cot to show me some boring artifacts covered by dusty plexiglass. The sign-in book informed me I was the first visitor in 3 days. But the ground outside was just fascinating.

It seemed to be made up more of thin, delicate potsherds than earth!! I walked myself around the open excavations, mentally checking off another pilgrimage site, before moving on. Since that time, better candidates for humanity's first settled village have been identified.

Also inland in the deepening snow I checked out Konya, where for thousands of years the locals carved dwellings and churches and mosques into the soft tufa stone of the surrounding hills. Not far away, an impromptu tour of Kaymakli underground city was provided by an enterprising guard, and the place was quite amazing. One ventilation/well shaft went down and down through 50 levels of subterranean habitations. In troubled times the people living in the local area above would hide in the underground city. The limited access of the entrances made it easy to defend, and unattractive to marauders.

A wacky French-speaking truck driver took me to the Syrian border while busily talking me out of various interesting coins, my broken flashlight, and breath freshener, before he actually TOOK my little silver/ruby heart charm found alongside the road, long ago in Italy. I waited until he stopped the truck and tried to exit, when I scooted hard across the cab bench seat, pinning his far arm between myself and the still-closed door. From there I had leverage enough to retrieve my silver charm from his vest pocket, mostly without his agreement, but we didn't come to blows over it. For reasons I didn't understand, the driver wanted everything I possessed. I was glad to leave his brand of 'crazy' behind at the border. I eventually gave that romantic silver charm ("My heart is yours" in Italian) to my new bride when we honeymooned in Italy in 1985.

Syria

Immigration and customs to Syria was accomplished without incident, and a Dutch truck carried me all the way into the center of Aleppo. The citadel there is picturesque, and I was startled to find St George's tomb, (yes, St. George the Dragon Slayer, patron saint of England) just inside the gateway of Aleppo's citadel.

Aleppo Citadel

From the town of Homs I got a short ride out east towards the ruins of Palmyra. When the driver realized where I was really going, he took me all the way to Palmyra, about 400 km round trip out of his way!! That seemed excessively generous of him, and I felt guilty. In Palmyra I for the ONLY time in all of my vagabonding, turned down a lodging house for being just too dirty. The partially reconstructed ruins looked nice.

Leaving Palmyra to return towards Damascus I found myself hiking along the road, and spotted some genuine Bedouin whose black tent was set up about 100 yards from the verge. Three women and three boys were there, plus infants. They called me over to visit and made me welcome, serving me some tea. The kids 'baksheeshed' (begging for a tip) me shamelessly, and I took out my flatbreads to share with everyone. When I tried to photograph the group, the women calmly turned their backs on the camera, but not in a mean way. They explained to me that their husbands wouldn't like it if I carried away a photo of their faces. I was quite pleased that my improving command of Arabic was able to understand that nuanced message.

Bleak Campsite

True Bedouin

Not far from Homs sits the castle called Krak des Chevaliers, the largest and most important castle in the middle east. Climbing through the various layers of battlements, one comes to understand why it was considered virtually impregnable.

Krak des Chevaliers

From Damascus it took only 2 rides to the door of the Youth Hostel in Amman, Jordan. In Amman I shuttled around to various embassies applying for visas to Saudi Arabia, Kuwait and Iran.

Archaeology in Jordan

I remembered my surprise in Nairobi about a year earlier when I had entered my cheap dorm at the Iqbal ("EEK-bahl") hotel to see a woman lying facedown on the low bed across the room. She wore a very short red dress displaying unusually long legs clad in nylons. I hadn't seen anything like Maureen in a long, long time. She and her husband Doug lived in Chicago, and didn't really have any schedule for their vagabonding. We parted with the standard "Well, maybe see you in Katmandu!" salutation.

And here they were in the Amman, Jordan hostel!! That dwelling was very comfortable, and after a few days relaxing and applying for the visas, I let myself be recruited by Maureen and Doug, who had local contacts at the university. Their acquaintance, an American archaeologist named Mark, solicited volunteer help to carry forward a very ambitious archaeological survey of the entire Jordan River valley. The three of us volunteered and recruited a few others at the youth hostel. Early Thursday we field-walker-volunteers collected on campus with a half-dozen Jordanian Archaeology students.

A mini-van and a Land Rover took us all out to our assigned piece of arid ground. The Jordanians wanted to sing, and after teaching us a couple of simple songs, requested that we teach them

Archaeological Survey

an American song. The first few we attempted didn't excite them, obviously not what they had in mind. I then broke into the upbeat, yodeling hillbilly song "They Call it that Good Old Mountain Dew" which seemed to be exactly the American song they desired!

Once we arrived at the piece of barren terrain to be surveyed, Mark trained us in what to look for and what to collect in our sample bags. We formed a single line spaced about 100 feet apart, and began walking slowly northeastward, hunting potsherds or other possible artifacts, keeping our neighbors on either side in sight. That worked fine for over an hour, but then I spotted seashell fossils in the limestone bedrock of a outcrop in my sector. I've always been fascinated by fossils, and so stopped there to collect a few nice samples, but apparently got distracted, and when I looked up, not a single person was anywhere in sight. I had managed to be left behind. After 20 minutes of pushing forward to try to catch up, I came to the foot of an abrupt saddle-shaped ridge which was just COVERED with potsherds. Climbing slowly, I put a few dozen of the most interesting pieces in my sample bag. Nearing the top I found a sherd which, unbelievably, was WET on one side. Raising my head I met the bemused eyes of a dozen Jordanian soldiers looking down at me. They had dug defensive trenches on this ridge, had broken one of their water-jars only moments before and thrown the pieces down the slope! The soldiers told me they had seen the rest of the field-walkers disappear generally to the east, so I turned to continue in that direction.

I followed the sound of a Land Rover horn and soon handed over my bag of finds. I had been outside the area we were supposed to sweep, but Mark the archaeologist said nobody had identified 'my' site before. He officially recorded it, attaching its code number to my sample bag. Local people told Mark that 'my' barren hill had always been called 'The Mill'.

The local folks also identified another unremarkable ridge as 'The Castle', so we drove over there to evaluate the site. Plenty of potsherds were found all over 'The Castle', which was already marked on the survey maps. There were no walls standing above ground level, but the foundations were still in-situ. I kicked along the aligned edges of a series of foundation stones for the walls and gatehouse of that site to make them stand out. Mark didn't know much about military history, and seemed pleased to have me present a short seminar as I revealed the outline of the sophisticated gatehouse, and the two right-angle turns in the entryway where attackers could be trapped and ambushed.

We sat in the vehicles in late afternoon, satisfied with our walking survey work. Mark stood on the track talking with an older gentleman who had arrived accompanied by a donkey. The old gent began to animatedly hop back and forth loudly shouting "BAH!!, BOH!!", holding his hands over his ears. I learned later that he was telling a story from late 1917 when British General Allenby's soldiers fired artillery to drive the Turkish army northward.

The Rose City

I looked forward to seeing the 'Rose City of Petra', hidden away in a remote area of eastern Jordan. A long truck ride dropped me off at the turnoff leading there, and before long a second truck pulled over and indicated that I should hop into the open back of the covered bed. There I discovered a couple of young Germans who also had their sights set on Petra. The truck clung to the twisting road through foothills then took a long right curve. To the west the entire sky was alight with various colors like flame! This was the most beautiful sunset I have ever seen, and we only were permitted to view it for a few seconds before the road turned back the other direction and the truck sides blocked our vista.

Twilight meant that it was too late to walk through the famous Siq ("Seek") today, so I chatted up the teashop owner and arranged for the three of us to sleep there overnight for a very small fee. Although I made it clear that I did NOT want to be locked in for the night, that's exactly what the proprietor did. Gunter, Freida and I decided which of the walls we would attempt to break through if a fire should threaten us in the night.

The SIQ

In the morning I took my backpack along through the extremely picturesque Siq ("Seek"), a very narrow passage through the intervening sandstone ridge to reach the ancient sites of Petra. At the time there was zero tourist infrastructure at Petra, no restrooms, cafes or souvenir stands, simply a pair of uniformed guys in the ticket kiosk. The facades of ancient tombs welcomed me before a group of 15 Jordanian schoolgirls approached me hesitantly to try out the English they had been studying. A few minutes later, both of their teacher/chaperones went around the corner of the canyon, out of our line of sight. The boldest of the schoolgirls, and the only one wearing red, reached up on tiptoe to kiss me on the cheek, causing squeals of outraged delight from her classmates. Several of the others then found the courage to likewise kiss my cheeks. They were being VERY naughty. The most forward girl then surprised me with a lingering kiss full on my lips, which caused loud enough squealing that the chaperones reappeared to put the kibosh on any additional daring behavior.

Jordanian
Schoolgirls

I spent some time looking at the recently-found artifacts spread out for sale on some blankets and attended by Bedouin ladies. One gal presented two ancient bronze coins, so worn that no features or letters were visible, only head shapes. I bargained with her a bit, but she could tell I really didn't much want those coins and that the next Farangi (Western Foreigner) to visit would pay her more.

Walking pretty far out of the central area of the ruins, a view point revealed itself. Looking westward towards Israel one could see a dozen steep ridges, disappearing in the haze. Wonderful echoes replied when I called out. That is the best echo-location I have ever discovered. Tiring of the great echoes, I decided not to leave Petra that evening, as the shadows were already lengthening. I had a piece of flat bread in my backpack, and chose a small remote tomb near echo point as my lodging for the evening.

Externally the tomb was only a door and a carved niche. Internally it took the form of an 11 foot square chamber about 5 feet high, with low benches on either wall, all carved directly from the surrounding pink sandstone. The bodies would have originally lain on the benches. Standing at the doorway, the left upper back corner of the chamber showed a triangular opening where a layer of outside rock had cracked and slid off in the distant past. A column of bright moonlight already slanted across the chamber onto the floor beside the doorway. I ate my bread sitting at the doorway, then arranged my down sleeping bag on the right bench, with my feet towards the door.

Finest Ghost

Every few hours I would awaken enough to note that the column of moonlight had swept farther across the floor. In the wee small hours, I realized that there was a faint source of light from INSIDE the tomb, behind the column of moonlight. Rolling over I was treated to the sight of a fuzzy humanoid form, glowing pale green, squatted down in the corner of the tomb under the triangular aperture. The face was indistinct. There was no sense of danger or threat. The ghost was paying me no mind. Its attention was focused on some delicate manual project between its feet. Quite surprised, I rolled away again, concluding that I was probably dreaming. After convincing myself that I was finally awake, I rolled again to my right. The indistinct figure was still visible! It continued delicately manipulating something on the tomb floor in front of it, until, after a few more moments, the image faded out and disappeared.

Petra Tomb with the Best Ghost I've ever seen

Now, I am a dedicated believer in science, but I still am not able to explain what my eyes actually saw in the tomb that night. In all the years since, I've never witnessed a more definite ghostly presence.

In the morning, I left an offering of my aluminum plate in the niche outside the tomb. An hour's walk brought me back to the entrance to the Siq. The same Bedouin lady I had bartered with yesterday came up to me and unwrapped something from a small piece of burlap. It was an ancient coin, but much less worn and more pristine than the previous samples. A lovely stylized image of an owl was on the reverse. I had read that the Owl was a symbol associated with the Nabatean civilization which had built the beautiful ruins at Petra. After some negotiation that ancient mystery owl found its way into my pocket as a souvenir of the Rose City of Petra.

To 'Disneyland'

In the Arab countries surrounding Israel it was unwise to show any indication that you had ever spent time in the Jewish State. Only Jordan allowed backpackers exit from and entry to Israel. An Israeli stamp in your passport would cause a refusal to be admitted to any of the others. The Israeli's knew this, and used a loose printed piece of paper that they would stamp in and out, and fold into your passport. That paper could be destroyed immediately after leaving the country. In Syria or Egypt, or Saudi Arabia, backpackers would use the puerile code word "Disneyland" in place of "Israel". In my journal each morning, instead of Jerusalem, I wrote "Amman" as my location, to avoid possible future problems.

I made my way to the notorious Allenby bridge border crossing between Jordan and Israel. My papers were judged good, but the Israeli border official, with his broad New Jersey accent, was suspicious of me after he discovered the Palestinian head cloth among my belongings. I received the most thorough search I've ever suffered. My stick deodorant was run entirely out of its case and broken to check inside it. A coarse comb was used to comb through my long hair. Every seam and corner of my backpack and all of my stuff bags were closely examined. Finally I was permitted to enter Israel. It pleased me greatly that even this extreme search had failed to find the backpack hiding place which I used often to smuggle currency.

The attitude of the average Israeli man was much less liberal than I had expected. In the USA, most Jews are solidly on the Left edge, politically, but in Israel I got plenty of flack about my long hair, and several times a day while hitch-hiking, drivers would flip me the middle finger as they passed without stopping. There definitely seemed to be more of a Redneck ethos to the average Israeli.

Jerusalem

I made my way to Jerusalem, and sought out "Mr. A's" hostel, owned by a fatherly Armenian man and centrally located inside the old city wall. It was a comfortable, inexpensive, friendly place, with plenty of backpackers in residence. There are lots of interesting things to see in Jerusalem, the 'big 3' probably being the Wailing Wall, the Dome of the Rock, and the Church of the Holy Sepulcher. What an amazing city, very holy for different reasons to three of the world's great religions.

Wailing
Wall

The Church of the Holy Sepulcher I found mesmerizing. There are six different Christian sects which have control or rights of passage over different bits of the sprawling, ramshackle Church. There were always a few rituals or processions taking place, day or night. Many chapels and obscure passageways could be seen. Processions, incense swingers, chanting, and dancing were going on continually in one part or another.

In the chapel of Golgotha I reached an index finger down through a bejeweled hole in the altar to touch the actual rock on which Jesus is believed to have been crucified.

Long before arriving in Jerusalem I had assigned myself a mission. I sought out the church territory of the Franciscans. From my reading, I had always admired the French leader of the successful first crusade, Godfrey of Bouillon. He managed to somehow hold the bickering crusading forces together long enough to capture Jerusalem, then refused to accept the title of King of Jerusalem, stating that no-one other than Jesus should claim the title. Wishing to honor Godfrey as one of my historical heroes, I made a contribution to the Franciscans and told them of my desire. Soon a smiling, fast-walking friar led me deeper into the private nether regions of the church. He unlocked the doors of a shallow cupboard attached to a supporting pillar. There they rested, Godfrey's 1000-year-old spurs and sword. The friar intuited my next desire, and handed me a pale gray handkerchief. This was wrapped around the sword hilt, then I lifted Godfrey's sword to my lips. Honoring Godfrey by kissing the pommel of his ancient sword fulfilled my pilgrimage.

The Museum of Israel was also located in the more modern part of Jerusalem. I perused the enormous numismatic collection there. After 45 minutes of careful search, a display case revealed the exact coin I had purchased in Petra, with the stylized owl image. The reverse of my coin was, surprisingly, even more perfectly preserved in detail than the sample on display. Rather than a Nabatean coin, it proved to be a Jewish coin from the reign of Herod, exactly the era of Jesus!! What a perfect souvenir!

A fascinating week was spent in and around Jerusalem. Returning across the Allenby Bridge to Jordan, I hitch-hiked southward all the way to the head of the Gulf of Aqaba, and slept on a gritty, windy beach there.

Meester Mostafa—Good?

Feeling satisfied with my sightseeing in Jordan, I decided to head east, through Saudi Arabia to Kuwait, and from there try to find some way across the Persian Gulf to Iran. I had acquired a Saudi transit visa in Amman. (Since non-Muslim tourists were discouraged from visiting the country, only a 'Transit' visa was possible.) A year earlier in Ethiopia I had attempted and failed to get a Saudi transit visa. I learned then that without possessing a vehicle of my own, a transit visa could not be obtained. In Amman, therefore, I lied when applying for the visa, inventing a license number for my imaginary vehicle. Chances were excellent that the Saudi officials would bounce me off the border when I showed up on foot.

There was only one way to find out. I rode a cheap bus to the outskirts of Amman, then stuck out my thumb. Six or seven short rides got me out to the eastern end of Jordan at a 'T' road junction where a teashop/bar was the only building anywhere in sight. Not many cars passed on the road to Saudi Arabia, maybe two every hour. I had a cup of tea in the bar, and the proprietor, when he learned where I was heading, told me that another patron, Mr. Mostafa, was returning to Saudi Arabia that very evening. He spoke with a short man wearing flowing white robes, a red checked headcloth and a Saudi black-head-dress-rope drinking at another table. Soon I was called over to meet Mr. Mostafa. Through the bar owner's translation we agreed that I would go back out to my hitching spot, and if I were still there when Mr. Mostafa finished his business, he would pick me up.

Returned to my thumbing spot, I realized that, foolishly, I still carried Israeli coins in my pocket! This could have marked me as a Jewish Spy, so I dug a small hole in the desert and buried seven coins for some future archaeologist to discover long after I'm gone.

An hour and a half later, a big, powerful gold-color Firebird muscle car stopped, rumbling forcefully. I hopped in the front seat to be immediately handed two open liter-bottles of beer, which I was to nursemaid and hand to the driver whenever he signaled to me. Whoops, dying in a car crash was NOT on my agenda for the evening, but I figured that with almost no traffic, MAYBE things would workout non-fatally. Mr. Mostafa only knew five words of English, but I got to hear all of them maybe 30 times over the course of the evening.

As we motored along, he often took his eyes off the road to look at me woozily.

"Meester Mostafa—Good?"

"Oh, yes, you are a great guy, Mr. Mostafa!"

"Meester Mostafa—Bad?"

"No, my friend, not Bad, everyone likes you."

"Meester Mostafa—Half and Half?"

Followed by gales of laughter at his joke in English.

But when we roared away and down the long, straight road east, I realized that Mr. Mostafa was not merely buzzed on beer (which wasn't available in Saudi Arabia) but was completely sloshed! He wasn't driving well at all, weaving from one edge of the blacktop to the other, and occasionally slipping off the road to blast along on the shoulder for a few seconds! We overtook one vehicle and passed it in a reckless manner. By this time sweat was running down my back between my shoulder blades and I was incredibly tense. Running off onto the shoulder again the hot Firebird dug its rear wheels into the sand and stuck there. Mr. Mostafa and I couldn't push it out, but a taxi driver and his fare kindly stopped to help get us back on the road. Mostafa was VERY unhappy to discover that both his bottles of beer had somehow emptied themselves onto the passenger seat floor. I apologized insincerely for not paying closer attention to his alcohol. At dusk as we continued eastward, the paved road made a 45 degree turn towards the north. Mr. Mostafa drove straight instead, which took us zooming out into the scrubby desert, not following any track, but steering around patches of bushes!

Hot Pontiac

"Whoa, Mr. Mostafa, the road is way back over there!"
"OK, Ok" He points ahead out into the darkness over which we rush, then ignoring our path, looking up through the windshield at the night sky he announces "Bedoueen!"
Yeah, right, you're a drunk Bedouin navigating by the stars across the trackless desert.

Now I'm quite terrified, because at sixty miles per hour, all we need is one shallow wadi (gully) and 'BAM!' we are both dead in a heartbeat. But after twenty minutes of terror, to my amazement, a light appeared on the faraway horizon directly ahead of us! Before long we stopped at an unsuspected border crossing with no roads leading up to it on the Jordanian side of the border. It seemed as though these backwater officials had never before seen a foreign passport. They welcomed me enthusiastically, stamped my visa with every stamp they possessed, and did

NOT ask to see the vehicle I supposedly owned! Lucky break. A well maintained road led away from the border post on the Saudi side, and soon I was sitting cross-legged on floor mats in Mr. Mostafa's modest house, drinking super-strong coffee poured over cardamom seeds. I never did catch a glimpse of his wife, she remained hidden in the other parts of the building. It had been a long day on the road, and I really just wanted to sleep, but soon men from the surrounding village began appearing at Mostafa's, being introduced to me, then sitting smoking, drinking coffee and chatting in his 20 x 20 foot sitting room.

"Happy to meet you, Mr. Mayor! And you, too, Mr. Chief of Police."

When about 20 guys had assembled, Mostafa casually stood up and moved towards the outside door, causing an immediate end to all conversation. He reappeared carrying a cardboard box full of bottles of Whiskey, to joyful acclaim. Apparently Mr. Mostafa was the local liquor smuggler, and the whole village proceeded to get rip-snorting, falling-over drunk on his 'imports'. These particular Muslims didn't take the Islamic proscription against alcohol very seriously.

I did finally get some sleep, and in the morning my hung-over friend Mostafa drove me out to the main road south, and dropped me off. I would really love to include my photo of Mr. Moustafa standing proudly beside his hot Pontiac, but after all these years, that might still embarrass him. So I have cartooned that image, and changed his name to be able to include the tale.

Hitching in Saudi Arabia

The road southeast to Riyadh and Kuwait ran parallel to a major oil pipeline for over 500 miles. Drivers understood about hitch-hiking, but had seldom seen anyone actually thumbing.

I was treated to a big dust storm, which kicked up the gritty desert surface in such quantity, that from time to time I couldn't see my own feet. I stood beside the road, my head wrapped up, peering through a slit in my head cloth as vehicles crept past with their headlights on. One pulled to the side of the road and viewed me up close. Three Saudis indicated I should climb in to the back seat, then asked me a few questions in Arabic, which I didn't understand, but tried in Arabic to answer appropriately. The Mercedes reversed course and began driving slowly back the way it had come! "Hey", I'm going THAT (pointing) way!" The driver told me something unfriendly and gruff, so I decided I'd just go along with them. It was easier to breathe in the car than out in the dust storm. They drove me back 5 miles and turned me in at the police station, seeming impressed with themselves. "Look, we found this terrorist out beside the oil pipeline!" The police checked my passport, determined I was allowed to be there, and released me. By then the dust storm was much diminished. My buddies in the Mercedes drove me back to exactly where they had found me, ejected me from their car, and drove on their way.

I caught a very good long ride in a Toyota pickup with a guy who, if he was telling the truth, was the Official Palace Artist in Riyadh. He had samples of his work in the bed of the truck. They were very reminiscent of the portraits I had seen applied to velvet at the Mexican border crossing in Tijuana.

I got a good look at the local Bedouin as we approached Kuwait. The tents were multicolored and mass produced for camping. Television antennae sprouted from the tents, with new, shining Cadillacs and Land Rovers parked all around. It was a perfect image of my fantasy of an encampment of very wealthy Bedouin.

Kuwait

A clinic in Kuwait City was thrilled to draw and bank my 'O-Negative' blood, paying me $33.50, which extended my traveling budget by over five days.

There was a clean, modern youth hostel in Kuwait City, and staying there was FREE! Still, only a few travelers were taking advantage of the lodging. My first glimpse of the Persian Gulf was not encouraging. The city harbor was oily and full of float-

Dhows on the Persian Gulf

ing rubbish. Dhow style watercraft clustered thickly there, each small vessel powered by a diesel truck engine.

Since all of Kuwait was a duty-free port, I purchased two cartons of the most expensive Players cigarettes, intending to sell them for a profit once inside Iran.

The plan was to ride across the gulf to Iran, then hitch-hike to the east through Afghanistan and Pakistan to India. I talked to a dozen dhow owners before finding one who would leave that evening headed for Abadan. That port lies some hundred miles up the Shatt al Arab, which is the river which empties into the gulf after the Tigris and Euphrates rivers combine with one another in Iraq. We agreed on a price for the ride, deck passage. The crew consisted of seven scrawny, feeble-looking older Iraqis. Four used passenger vehicles had been somehow placed on the deck, and were destined for Abadan.

Just Another Pilgrim on the Dhow to Iran

We chugged out into the gulf at dusk, and into the teeth of a freshening wind. This particular dhow's steering system was not reassuring. The skipper sat in the wheelhouse at the stern with his feet resting on the shoulders of one of the crew sitting blind below him, and holding the tiller. When the skipper wanted to change direction he tapped his foot on one shoulder or the other, and the helmsman made the correction without being able to see ahead.

The storm caught us, rocking the dhow violently and dumping heavy squalls of rain on me. I was soaked through almost immediately, and the things in my pack were also getting wet. Discover-

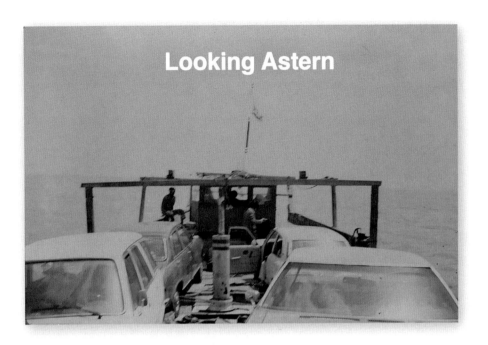

Looking Astern

ing that a cargo Chevrolet coupe was unlocked, I looked aft to see the skipper kindly waving me inside the vehicle. Blasted full of Dramamine, and deliberately empty of food, I didn't suffer much from sea-sickness, and got some sleep on the rear seat. During the worst part of the storm, the violent rocking of the vessel caused my Chevrolet to 'walk' itself a few feet across the deck and punch its right rear tire down through the central hatch-cover. The jury-rigged ropes and tie-downs used to secure the vehicles were poorly thought out and much too flimsy for the purpose.

In the morning the storm had passed, and all was calm. We had anchored in the lee of an offshore island, and this protection had served us well. The crew worked to haul up the anchor, but it was a laborious grind, and only progressed slowly. I added my strong back to the task and the anchor came up twice as fast. The scrawny crewmen smiled happily at me, and later gave me tea and some nice soup in thanks for teaming up with them. I hadn't brought any food, as the trip was supposed to take only 15 hours, but we had already wasted that long dealing with the storm, so it was good luck that the crew accepted me as an honorary member.

The gulf seemed to be just FULL of lovely flying fish!! They would appear on both sides of the bow, launching themselves and extending their wings, while the powerful, busy tails propelled them along above the surface at high speed. One or more sharks were almost always visible just under the surface of the gulf.

Sailing northward in perfect weather, the crewmen started screaming at one another, rushing fore and aft with arms gesticulating. I wasn't worried, as similar scenes were enacted whenever even a routine, simple task was to be accomplished. But then, dark gray smoke issued from the engine room hatch! We had a fire onboard!! Soon chunks of burning wooden boards were thrown up out of the hold onto the deck, to be collected by me and others and thrown overboard. Since we were completely out of sight of any shore, I began deciding how I might turn my backpack into a float. But a moment later the burning wood quit appearing and the smoke dissipated. The fire was out, and we could proceed.

Smugglers

We entered the brown water at the mouth of the Shatt al Arab and motored up the wide river against the current. Many fishermen had their nets placed across the flow of the river, and when the skipper turned the dhow to avoid running across the nets, fishermen would throw a fish on board in thanks.

We tied up to another of the forty or so dhows which all clustered around the immigrations and customs barge which was anchored in the middle of the channel. The skipper began jumping from boat to boat to present his paperwork to the authorities. Approval was a slow process, but finally completed at sunset. The customs officials boarded our craft proceeding to lock down all of our luggage and all storage spaces on board with short wire cables affixed with lead 'crush' seals. I discovered that one of the crew had put a pair of new shoes in the top of my backpack without clearing it with me first. I angrily pretended to throw the shoes overboard, then gave them back to their owner. I dug through my backpack to assure myself that nothing else new had been added. The customs guy then wired the compartments of my pack shut and used a plier-like hand seal to secure the wire.

Proceeding upriver in the dark, the crewmen were very busy digging various items out of obscure hiding places, and stacking them carefully in the center of an enormous tarpaulin spread out on the center of the deck. New clothing and shoes, Liquor bottles, cartons of cigarettes, and all manner of other contraband were being collected.

We made a sudden 90 degree right turn towards the Iranian riverbank. Once inshore as closely as we could travel, six men materialized out of the dark palm forest onshore, and waded up close to the dhow. The crew then rolled the 'contraband ball' about 10 feet in diameter, over the gunwale and onto the shoulders of the gents waiting in the shallow water. The 12-legged creature scurried up the bank and into the darkness. Without knowing, I had purchased passage on a dedicated SMUGGLER'S DHOW!

Roaming Asia

In the early morning we moored to many other dhows stacked up in the harbor at Abadan. The boats between us and the dock were jammed with deck passengers, and I felt very fortunate that I had enjoyed so much space on our vehicle-carrying dhow.

Two Iranian immigration officials appeared on the dock about 8 am. Since they could see me easily, and I was an unusual arrival, the officials pointed to me signaling 'come here'. I shook hands with the skipper and all of my crew buddies, donned my still-sealed pack and climbed across four intervening dhows, effectively 'jumping the queue' of hundreds of immigrants. The highest ranking uniformed Iranian led me into the large customs shed, and to a lonely table at the far end. He checked the seals on my backpack, finding them undefiled, and cut them off. Looking over my passport he asked if I had anything to declare. I started to pull a carton of cigarettes out of my bag, whereupon he turned his head away exclaiming "Don't show me that, DON'T SHOW me that!"

Again "Do you have anything to declare"
"No, nothing".
My passport was stamped for entry and I was admitted to Iran. When exiting I left behind one pack of cigarettes as backsheesh for my helpful immigration official.

Immediately outside of the customs building I sold all of my remaining cigarettes to an eager tout. A profit of $11.40 USD was achieved, which expanded my traveling money by two more days. The morning weather was good so I moved into a tatty local public park and draped all of my wet clothing and belongings over a bush, to dry them out in the wan sunshine. Young men congregated to laugh at me and tease me a little bit, but soon were lured into friendly conversation.

Drying Out

To Persepolis

Wanting to see the ruins of Persepolis, I hitched onto the main road in that direction. But the entire countryside was, for reasons I still haven't learned, underwater at the time. The knee-deep water flowed steadily from North to South across our direction of travel. Big trucks could still move around on the roads, but they tended to slide off and become bogged in the surrounding mud. I volunteered to help out by wading ahead of 'my' truck to locate the edges to the pavement. After several hours we drove up out of the flood, and the truckers made room for me in the cab.

Persepolis is really worth a visit. At that time a new theory was gaining credibility, claiming Persepolis was NOT a palace, but rather a ceremonial site which was used only occasionally.

From beautiful Persepolis I had a few short rides before an architecture student named Masood picked me up and drove me all the way to Teheran!!

Welcome to Teheran!

Finally in Teheran, Masood dropped me off at 3 am in some random residential area. I decided to get some shut-eye and then figure things out in the morning. There were no sidewalks between the rubbished road and the walls of the various family compounds all around, and I really didn't want to get run over by a vehicle. One compound was surrounded by 8-foot-high walls, but had an entry gate which was lower. I looked in to see a small area of grass surrounded by garden flowers. Reaching WAY over the gate I tried the latch, and it admitted me. Figured I could get 3 hours sleep, then be up and away long before the owners awoke, so I deployed my ground cloth and sleeping bag.

But no, my timing was way off. It was already light before I awoke, groggy, to the sound of footsteps approaching from the direction of the residence. Oof, there I was, flagrantly trespassing. Decided to pretend to stay asleep, and tensed up my back for the imminently-expected kick! But strangely—the footsteps could now be heard retreating towards the house. I rolled half over to discover a tray had been set down beside my head. Bread, Feta cheese, walnuts, sliced tomatoes and cucumber, along with some nice green herbs were presented for my breakfast, along with a small glass of hot Persian tea. Welcome to Teheran!

After enjoying my morning repast I wrote a short note of thanks, and left it on the tray with a little souvenir of the USA. I carried tiny glass bottles each created around a shiny new Lincoln penny, to give away whenever it seemed appropriate.

Finding my way into the center of town, I booked a bed in a big, impersonal guest-workers dormitory. Nearly all of the other residents were Koreans, earning money to send home to their families.

Iran's central museum was full of interesting exhibits. I viewed the famous Peacock throne, completely covered with precious stones. Its decoration was much too 'busy' for me to consider it beautiful.

I made a bad mistake by eating a little prepared sandwich from a street vendor. It tasted 'off' so after one bite I threw the remainder away. That night I really paid the price, as the case of food-poisoning took me into territory more violently ill than I have ever been in my life. I spent actual hours dry-heaving into one of the guest house toilets while Korean neighbors abused me verbally for stinking up the facilities.

When I was ready to leave Teheran, I hitch-hiked north over the low mountains surrounding the Caspian Sea. There the terrain was much more green and fertile than in the southerly areas of Iran. My penultimate ride in Iran took me nearly to the border of Afghanistan. As I opened the door to leave the driver demanded money to cover his petrol costs. Free rides were the cultural norm to the west of that point, but from there eastward everyone is expected to pay for any transport until hitch-hiking gratis becomes again possible in Malaysia.

I heard an interesting story at this mountain border crossing. The Iranian soldiers stationed in the border encampments would occasionally suffer casualties to raiding parties of Afghans. The local commander complained to Teheran that his soldiers needed upgraded, modern weapons in order to hold their own against the stealthy tribesmen. When they were re-equipped with wonderful new FAL automatic rifles, however, their losses to raiders instantly quadrupled!! The Afghans, you see, liked and desired those modern rifles, and were quite willing to murder an Iranian conscript to get one.

Asian Prisons

First printed in 1975, a book called *South East Asia on a Shoestring* codified quite a bit of overland traveler lore and information, including plenty of advice on how to organize the inside of your head for super-low-budget travel. Perhaps the most interesting idea was that if an innocent traveler was unlucky, it was easy to find oneself incarcerated for long periods of time, and that the overland traveler community should support those unlucky souls. I took this to heart, and, finding myself in eastern Iran's biggest city, Mashhad, I solicited a permission letter from the governmental prosecutors allowing me to visit the Zendan prison. I took a bus to the outskirts of town, walked quite a distance to find the prison entrance, and asked to see the foreign prisoner who had gone the longest time without a visitor.

The prison guards soon presented an American named Jay. In the Afghan language the number 8 is pronounced "Hasht", so Jay was serving Hasht years for attempting to smuggle Hasht kilos of Hash Hish. The US Embassy in Teheran was aware of him, and had visited him when he was first incarcerated. He seemed to be clean and healthy, and was pleased when given the 3 most recent Newsweek magazines plus some nice oranges and apples I had brought for him. When asked if there was anything I could do for him, Jay immediately started writing a list. "Yes, that would be great, downtown there is the 'American Store', and I'd like a ham, 10 cans of corned beef, bread, coffee, peanuts, cheese, and 40 chocolate bars." Just as I was wondering how I could afford to perform this favor, Jay pulled a GIANT roll of Iranian Rial bills out of his pocket, peeling off two high-denomination notes for me to spend. In discussions thereafter I learned that entrepreneurial Jay had used money from his parents to set up a tourist-trinket-manufacturing operation there inside the prison. He claimed 40% of the Zendan inmates were his employees making beadwork-decorated leather bracelets, belts and similar items, selling them to a distributor who passed them on to tourist shops. Jay was doing just fine for money, most of which he was banking outside the prison awaiting his release. He wasn't the impecunious, despairing, beaten-down prisoner I had expected to meet.

Traveling back into town I found myself walking behind a couple of low-budget overland vagabonds who looked familiar. I had originally met Californians Kurt Hanselman and Vicki Fong in Spain four months previously. When we each learned that the others intended to head east through Asia, we said, jokingly, "—well, see you in Asia". Now there we were. I searched everywhere for the 'American Store', finally concluding that it was only a phantom. I used Jay's money to buy all of his luxury foods at other import stores, and delivered them to Jay two mornings later. He seemed glad that I had bought additional chocolate bars to use up every rial of the money he had handed me.

Cheap Turquoise

Mashhad is seventy miles south of the world's biggest turquoise mine, and is therefore probably the cheapest place on the planet to purchase turquoise. I looked in on many shops in the covered souk, and finally worked the prices down enough that I spent an entire afternoon sorting through the turquoise offerings of the shop which had high quality stones and, if one purchased in bulk, the best prices. My plan was to carry the stones to Indonesia, where they could be sold for a substantial profit.

Into Afghanistan

The joys of Iran were paling so I boarded the minibus which ran from Mashhad to Herat, some distance on the Afghan side of the border. I bought a ticket only to the border itself, not all the way to Herat. This was considered foolish and commented on by the other dozen foreign vagabonds already on board. I cleared both Iranian outgoing and Afghan entry customs easily, and walked ¼ mile along the main road to Herat before a truck stopped and nego-tiated a tiny price for the ride into town. Checking in to the first random lodging on Herat's main street (still unpaved at that time) I found it to be lovely, airy, cheap, and welcoming. I was strolling along that street three hours later when the minibus finally arrived, having been detained by waiting for the slowest-clearing of the passengers. Afghanistan in 1976 was really a paradise for low-budget vagabonds. Everyone had plenty to eat, and hashish was available at unbelievably low prices. The locals were very calm and well centered, welcoming the only sort of tourists they knew.

The Green Chador

I learned a little bit of Pashtun, the local language, and was strolling a side street saying 'Good morning, how are you?' to everyone I met. All of the local women were wearing the Chador, a

Six Men Hammering

Camel Market

Butcher Shop

sort of ankle length tent over their heads with a nearly opaque piece of mesh over the eyes. I greeted a dark green chador, and it came to an immediate stop. I paused. There was SOMETHING going on under the chador, and suddenly a young woman's BEAMING face appeared from underneath. "Fine thanks, how are you?" she said, then again dropping the hem of her garment. At the time I thought this was very kind. She knew that western women did not hide their faces, and since I was willing to speak to her in Pashtun, she met me halfway and revealed her face to me. Then I began to worry, looking over my shoulders to assure myself that her brothers had not witnessed her temerity.

I spent a pleasant week in Herat. The Afghans had perfected a technique by which they could 'roast' small quantities of hashish so that it would burn dandy by itself, not needing to be rolled with shredded tobacco. After a cheap meal in a restaurant I was handed one of these cigarettes, gratis, for dessert, and badly misjudged its potency. I found that I had to continually scrape my fingers against the rough stucco wall just to maintain myself with some reliable sensory input. Had a hard time finding my way back to the hotel, and really didn't enjoy being out of control, so I swore off any intoxicants for quite a few months afterward.

Shepherds

A truck ride to Kandahar, the next big city of Afghanistan was secured. I enjoyed riding up on top of the cab until the owners brought me down due to "Police". We drove slowly and safely for almost 14 hours before I could climb out of the stuffy cab and fill my lungs with air uncontaminated by diesel fumes.

Afghan Transport

In Kandahar a tailor helped me buy a bus ticket on to Kabul, then forced me to admire everything in his shop, pressuring me to purchase something. I agreed that he could make me a shirt for 60 cents, but that wasn't good enough, and he proceeded to become more and more aggressive and menacing. Two cousins appeared and supported him in the 'discussion'. Finally I stood up, declaring that his shitty attitude had made me decide that I would do no business with him at all. I stepped forward and shoved the tailor back a step, preparing to fight my way to the street, but then the three of them laughed and pretended that it had all been a joke, and lied that they were just kidding around. No one followed me back to my lodging, which I considered a blessing.

Once in Kabul I found myself a room on Chicken Street and again bumped into my friends Kurt and Vicki. They had confirmed the existence of amazing Korean Air Lines tickets from Bangkok to

California for only $300, and allowing unlimited stopovers on the way there. Their plan HAD been to travel East to Afghanistan, then back West to Istanbul, where they had left much of their luggage, returning to the US through Europe. The KAL tickets changed their plan to continuing east, and across the Pacific to home. Kurt was about to head back to Istanbul to collect all of their stored stuff, and Vicki arranged with me to watch out for her while Kurt was away. You see, Vicki had a head of Gorgeous Raven-blue/black thigh-length hair which pretty much fried the libidos of all Afghan males. The Afghan girls were compelled to always hide away their hair, so Vicki was always an object of intense interest wherever we went in Afghanistan. Ultimately, I succeeded at keeping Vicki un-molested until Kurt reappeared.

Vicki and I found the blood clinic in Kabul, and lined up with hundreds of Afghan men. When the officials saw us they jumped us up in the queue because they wanted our locally-unusual blood types. The nurses admired Vicki's hair, and made disparaging

Gorgeous Hair

comments about mine. They drew the blood from my earlobe!! It didn't hurt, and I was given 600 afghanis (about $12 USD) in payment, which increased my traveling funds by over two days on the road.

Prison Visit Redux

Saturday was visiting day at Bagram, the main prison on the outskirts of Kabul. I put my 3 most recent copies of Newsweek magazine in a brown paper bag with 5 big oranges, and Vicki and I bussed to the prison. The scene was very strange. The prison was huge, hundreds of single-story barracks surrounded by a very high razor wire fence. Thirty feet outside that fence was another fence made of iron bars between masonry pillars. On visitor's day two Afghan soldiers with loaded automatic weapons sat on each masonry pillar, one looking down on the fence at each side. When the gates of the inner fence were opened, the prisoners could come out into the gap between the fences while the visitors were free to walk up to the outer fence. I used my 20 words of Pashtun to communicate with some of the incarcerated Afghans, and pretty soon they fetched out a German and a Frenchman who were inmates. They both seemed to be doing fine, and their respective embassies were working to secure their imminent release. But they told me about an Italian vagabond who had arrived the day before. That guy spoke only Italian and was freaking out. He had already tried twice to run and climb the fence to escape, and my informants were sure that he would be shot upon the next attempt. I agreed to try to get this information to the Italian diplomats.

Now, though, I wanted to pass my bag of magazines and oranges through the metal bars to the vagabonds on the inside, but wasn't sure this was allowed. I tried to ask the soldiers sitting up on top of each masonry pillar, but couldn't get their attention. Naturally, ALL of the Afghan men for 50 yards in any direction were gazing with great longing at Vicki who stood just behind my shoulder. "Vicki, would you please go over there" (50 feet away) "and brush out your hair?" She did so, and I gave the package to the prisoners. Nobody paid ANY attention, I could have passed them a Rocket Launcher!

When we arrived back into the center of Kabul, I fed some coins into a public telephone. I had never used a phone in Asia before that moment. I was very lucky and shortly was connected with an English-speaking operator. I explained what I needed, and to my complete astonishment, I soon found myself speaking to the Italian Ambassador himself at home on his day off (!) Impossible, I know. The ambassador spoke no English nor French, so I had to use my 40 words of Italian to deliver the message.

"Italian Man—Bagram prison—BIG danger!"
"You Go Bagram prison TODAY, NOW, very important TODAY, NOW, see Italian Man."

The Ambassador repeated my instructions in perfect Italian, seemed to understand what was needed and to be leaving immediately for the prison. So I think it very likely that Vicki and I did a serious good turn for the poor terrified Italian prisoner.

To Bamian

Vicki and I rode an inexpensive bus to the Bamian valley, checking in to the cheap Wanderer hotel. Bamiyan's ancient, huge, famous Buddha statues, carved out of the cliffs overlooking the

Bamian Valley

Atop the Head
of the
Great Buddah

Great Buddah

town, were impressive. We went into the honeycombed tunnels in the surrounding cliff, and found our way after much trial and error, to the top of the Great Buddha's head, where Vicki posed for a photograph. Since the Taliban with Chechen help destroyed both of the Buddhas in 2001, this photo-op no longer exists.

Another nearby antiquity was visited 30 miles past Bamian town. 800 years earlier, the armies of Genghis Kahn conquered and sacked a large mud-brick-built city, killing or enslaving every inhabitant. The ruined city is still there, slowly eroding back into the earth.

Abandoned City

Afghanistan in 1976 was a wonderful place for low-budget vaga-bonds. After I had protected my friend Vicki Fong from as many vagabonding perils as I could, she finally had to bus back to Kabul to meet her boyfriend Kurt, returning from Istanbul. The Afghan guys at the 'Wanderer' lodging in Bamiyan were sad to see her go.

I banded together with a half-dozen other vagabonds to rent a small 4wd truck to view the ethereal beauty of vivid-blue lakes further into the mountains at Band-i-Amir. There I met and chatted up a Kiwi gal named Linda Hill who had somehow man-aged to vagabond ALONE through Turkey, Iran, and much of Afghanistan. Linda was completely fed-up with being continu-ally harassed and threatened by Muslim men, who just couldn't

Band i Amir

Curious
Men

Photo by
Linda Hill

accept that she was not some man's property. She was ready to have somebody like me give her 'cover' and surcease from the continual harassment. We rode the same share truck back to Bamian. Our eyes locked as we stood together at the Wanderer Hotel's check-in desk. I raised my eyebrows, and Linda gave a curt nod. We were room-mates.

Power Over Women

The guys working at the Wanderer were VERY impressed with me, teaming up with another unattached young woman only days after releasing Vicki back to Kabul. Women traveling completely solo were quite rare, and they had noted Linda when she passed through Bamian earlier. Soon after checking in, Hap, the young owner of the Wanderer told me I must be sad that Vicki had departed for Kabul without me. The desk man, standing nearby, reported:

"Oh, he haas ah NOTH er WAN".

The boys then convinced themselves that I was the western vagabond they had been waiting for. Five of the local young men, including Hap, ambushed me in a corner of the courtyard, begging me to reveal to them the secret of compelling women to be my playthings. They knew there must be some secret phrase or incantation or touch or tune or gesticulation which would win them the affection of tourist women. I explained to them that in both cases, Vicki and I, and Linda and I, were merely traveling buddies, and had no sexual relationship, but of course, since we were in both cases sharing a room, they just flat-out refused to believe me.

"No, Truly my friends, in my heart it is as though I were a BROTHER to Vicki and Linda."

One guy then got a faraway look in his eye, and reported to the group what he had seen a week earlier when I opened the bedroom door to his knock. Over my shoulder he had glimpsed Vicki in her sleeping togs of only panties and a spaghetti-strap silk camisole. He didn't have the English for that, of course, but his Pushtun plus hand-gestures defining the outfit were easy to understand. This sighting was considered conclusive by the assembled young Afghans.

"We are nowt STUPID men, Mister Chick!"
"A Sister is nowt using this clothing at a Brother!"

The hormone-addled Afghan guys just couldn't reorganize their heads to accept young women as people first, and beddable possessions second. They were genuinely frustrated with me. I ultimately failed to convince them that I was not just being cruel to them by refusing to let them in on the secret.

Linda Hill

Linda turned out to be an excellent traveling partner. Whenever the situation went crazy, and things were wild and dangerous, and the shit was coming down, Linda would be hip-to-hip with me, stalwart, fearless, dealing with the problem. Then when things finally calmed down Linda would collapse and cry bitterly on my shoulder. The girl was smart, focused, and very capable. And she had a TEMPER. We traveled together for over a year (Afghanistan, Pakistan, India, Sri Lanka, Nepal, Burma, Thailand, Malaysia, Indonesia). After a few months I could tell exactly what type of behavior would trigger Linda's Fury. When we encountered such provocative behavior, I would simply turn away for a moment until "Linda's Lightning" struck, then re-engage to help pick up the pieces. As an added attraction, Linda always formed a mysterious instant bond with all the local women we encountered.

Pathanistan

Well up in the mountains which separate Afghanistan and Pakistan there exists a country which doesn't appear on any map. The map puts the territory of the fiercely-independent Pathan ("Pah-TAHN") tribes in either Pakistan or Afghanistan, but governmental control doesn't actually reach into the hills. Pakistan provides free electricity to Pathanistan, while Afghanistan provides free medical services in a well-understood unwritten arrangement which the Pathans honor by not raiding down into the plains.

In May of '76 we approached the Khyber Pass from the Afghan side. I had purchased a ride sitting on the hood of a very large, heavy, 1954 Chevrolet which climbed the switchbacks towards the saddle of the pass. A dozen Afghani men shared the hood, completely covering it. Linda was assigned a seat inside the vehicle. Once up in the hills we found ourselves in the quasi-sovereign nation of Pathanistan. We saw plenty of small, derelict fortresses on many hilltops, and rows of 'dragon's teeth' obstacles on the way up to the very highest point of the Khyber pass, where several bad roads headed off in different directions. A wheezing bus was headed a short distance along the ridge to the legendary smuggler town of Landi Khotal ("Lawn-dee-koh-TAHL"). Every seat was already claimed, so we climbed up the rear ladder to the huge luggage rack on top. Five men were already sitting on lug-

gage there. Three of them carried military-style rifles and bando-
liers of ammunition hung from their shoulders.

Mohammed Khasim's Hashish and Firearm Shop

As we climbed down to the rutted dirt main drag of Landi Khotal a man approached me with a welcoming smile, handed me
his card, and invited us into his business. The card informed me
that we were about to enter "Mohammed Khasim's Hashish and
Firearm shop."—what could possibly go wrong in a place like
that?? One big interior wall was completely covered by displayed
firearms, from tiny locally-manufactured 'pen pistols', illegal in
every country on earth, to a 13-foot long copy of an 20 mm Oer-
likon aircraft auto-cannon!!

"What would anyone want with a big, powerful automatic weapon like this, Mohammed Khasim??"
"This gun is very good to cut down the mud-brick walls of your
enemy's clan compound."

The Pathan gunsmiths were quite amazing, and could copy ANY
firearm, often including the manufacturer's model numbers and
proof marks. The copies were said to be quite robust and reliable,
but still, for the price of a single British-made .303 Short Magazine Lee-Enfield rifle, one could buy 2 of the local copies with
money left-over.

Mohammed Khasim kept insisting that if we planned to travel
around in the mountains, I MUST have a Sten submachine gun so
that I could protect myself and my companion. (It cost only $80,
iirc, and that was the starting price before bargaining, so it would

have been good value.) He finally quit pushing when I explained to him that we would be safer without a weapon. I really didn't want to have one over my shoulder when we inevitably met one of Mohammed Khasim's cousins who had always wanted a Sten gun, and happened to be carrying a long-range rifle.

He took us up the split-log stairs saying "I will show you something you have never seen before". I had been hearing that line ever since Tunisia, and it usually presaged a scam, but not this time.

The upstairs was only a single 12 x 12-foot room with two windows, and it contained nothing except two canvas folding cots, one of which had two open-topped cardboard boxes underneath it. These boxes appeared to be wet from the bottom, stained and shiny for about ⅔rds of their height. Mohammed K pulled one out, reached in with two fingers, and handed Linda a lump of resin-ey hashish about a centimeter in diameter. "There", he said, "that is for free, and if you finish it I will give you more."

Yowee, both boxes were soaked, not with water, but with the world's finest hash oil! Each box had 15 pounds of juicy new hash inside! The little room reeked of it, and I'm sure we were all getting high just from breathing the air there.

He had given the gift to Linda, not only because he liked her, but because I had sworn off dope. After the bad experience of overdosing on hash a month before in Herat, because of its completely unexpected potency, I was still shy of the stuff.

Linda swallowed a pea-sized chunk of new hash, giggling only a little bit. She had perhaps a little TOO MUCH faith in my ability to keep her safe while she was wasted.

"So", I said, "what is it that I will see which is new to me?"
"The hash presser is coming soon", said Mohammed Khasim.

The Hash Presser

During about 10 minutes of pleasant chat, I learned that the hash presser was a well-paid specialist who did nothing else for his living. There was some commotion downstairs, and a really powerfully built, short man in boots, bloused trousers, open vest and turban ascended the stairs carrying a wooden case. He was followed by several locals, all of whom seemed to be in business with Mohammed K in some fashion. There were two remarkable things about the hash presser. The first was his build, with shoulders much broader than his torso, and huge arms and neck. The more surprising thing was, though, that he wasn't wearing a shirt under his vest, showing off his powerful chest, shoulders, and arms. All of the other Moslem men in that part of the world were very shy about showing anything of their bodies except ankles, head and hands.

This character was introduced to us, and from his box, produced a small brass tray, and a brass balance with weights. He squatted on the floor next to one of the oily boxes of hash, and balanced the tray horizontally on his knees and stomach. His fingers selected an amount of the soggy hashish, choosing an amount which he modified by throwing back a small piece.

Mr. Hash P then held the blob of resin over the tray, cupped between his horizontal palms, with the fingers of each hand resting on or under the opposite wrist. He suddenly applied huge pressure, his shoulders bunching up and all the cords in his neck standing out, as he rotated his palms in opposite directions through 180 degrees. Purest dark colored hash oil ran in a small, steady stream from his hands into the tray, being collected by a groove around the edge into a corner recessed pocket. He opened his dull green palms and handed a dry pressed hash "cookie", fat in the center and thin around the edges, to Mohammed K who weighed each on the balance. This amazing display was then repeated dozens of times. The cookies were all of uniform weight to within half a gram of one another! Every four or five cookies the collected hash oil was decanted into a glass bottle from the receptacle at the corner of the tray.

Quite a performance, and a very interesting specialty.

I did a deal with Mohammed Khasim to fire some of his 'reloaded' ammunition with a Sten gun. I only paid for 10 rounds, though the magazine would hold 30. Behind the shop, cut out of the mountain slope was a small shooting range. I fired from the hip at a paper target, and had trouble controlling my aim. Unfortunately the reload ammunition wasn't good, and 2 of my ten rounds misfired, so even though Mohammed Khasim replaced the faulty cartridges, I never really got a satisfying burst out of the Sten gun.

From Landi Khotal we rode a rattletrap bus down the Eastern side of the Khyber Pass that same evening to the Pakistani border post. As we were navigating the various desks and getting the needed passport stamps a sly young man tried to sell us drugs BEFORE we cleared customs, but he was deflected. On the other side of the border waited a number of share busses to carry us on to Peshawar.

Bagpipes in Pakistan

A very crowded dirty downtown district welcomed us to a 5ᵗʰ floor guesthouse in Peshawar. The whole built-up block was a huge firetrap, so I walked about to identify all possible ways to

exit and descend, mapping them in my mind in case of a confla-
gration. After dark we heard a strange noise, increasing in volume
as it neared us in the street below. Two elephants carried the most
venerable members of a wedding procession, and in front of them
marched a pair of bagpipers!! The bride of the young military officer sat high in a howdah, almost completely hidden by the bejeweled golden necklaces with which she was encrusted.

Continuing to the huge, sprawling capital city of Lahore, we
visited the impressive Red Mosque, well worth a visit. We had
a tourist map of Lahore, but it wasn't really accurate enough for
navigation on foot. I soon learned NOT to unfold the map anywhere in Pakistan. That act always caused the collection of a
big crowd of local loungers who pressed forward, craning their
necks to see over my shoulder, with animated discussion among
our new admirers. Finally realized that the average Lahore resi-
dent had never before seen a map of his city, so it was extremely

interesting. Denied maps, then, how did we navigate? Not very well. By asking directions, and not ceasing until we had several corresponding answers in a row, we would then walk. Unfortunately, it seems that Pakistan cradles one of the cultures in which, if asked a question, not answering is considered impolite. So the average unsophisticated Pakistani simply invents an answer, and delivers it confidently, so as not to disappoint you.

Linda
and
New Friends

We made our way to see the beautiful old muzzle-loading cannon 'ZamZammeh', or 'Kim's Gun', just outside the Lahore museum, as made famous by Rudyard Kipling's novel KIM.

To Gilgit

Although the passes were still blocked by winter snows we decided to travel up into the northern mountains to visit storied Gilgit. We found a nice rest house in Abbotabad, and remained on the comfortable string-beds there both going north and returning south. A really gorgeous storm broke over Abbotabad. The lightning playing along the sheer ridges above the town was the best and most impressive ever I have seen. It was possible to see MORE THAN 10 lightning strikes per second for short periods.

Pathan Clothing

Sudden Death

In the dangerous mountain areas of Asia, there is much less assurance that one's life will continue. Riding a bus uphill in the outskirts of a small mud-brick town, I was sitting at the window with Linda beside me. Everyone heard a frantic shriek ahead!

A man loudly wailed "NAH—NAH—NAH—NAH!!!"

I glanced out the window to see a very gory sight. A body lay on the verge of the road with feet away from me. The entire top of his head was completely missing, down to below his eyes!! It had JUST occurred, and I watched the intact grey/pink brain slide out of the brain pan onto the tarmac, with blood welling up from the exposed spinal column!! I grimaced, and Linda moved across me to see. Holding her away, I recommended that she NOT take in the scene, and to my surprise, she agreed. The bus continued to move, and no explanation of the horrible accident was ever provided. The lesson, though, was very clear to me. We are very fragile bags of protoplasm, which can be casually dismembered in a heartbeat.

The international youth hostel map showed a location high in the mountains near a village named Sharan. We expected that it would be closed up for the season, but instead the caretaker opened the place up for us to be the only residents for a few days. We knew the passes were still blocked with deep snow, so lingered awhile in hopes the road would melt open.

Pathan Culture

In a temporary encampment only a quarter mile from the hostel was a lumber company which was harvesting all of the older Walnut trees in order to make cricket bats. The directors were interesting Pathan guys named Mr. Kareen Afridi and Mr. Bacha Afridi. The two men were not more closely related than at the Afridi clan level. Kareen had been educated in England, and spoke perfect English. He was a traditional boy in many ways, but understood intimately the differences between his Pathan culture and ours. For the three evenings following we allowed ourselves to be coddled by the Khyber Lumber Company directors who had their staff prepare wonderful dinners for us, and hosted fascinating discussions afterward.

Kareen's mother had demanded that he come home from the English University to be near her, and he did so, giving up all his plans to become a western banker. Kareen said his mom would never believe it if he were to tell her about a vagabonding couple who traveled together without being married. "So, I will not tell her!" I seemed to gain credibility with the Afridis by describing the workings of the ejection mechanism of the obscure British Martini-Henry rifle. We discussed the Pathan refusal to teach their girls to read. The directors freely admitted that it was so the women could not read the Koran for themselves. If they could read, the girls would discover that the men were lying when they affirmed that the Koran commands women to live under Purdah.

As a very young man, Kareen himself had participated in two clan vendettas and described for us how the operations were carried out. All the men of his Afridi sub-clan awoke at midnight and very quietly mounted up on their ponies. Dark capes covered their clothes, and rags were tied through any piece of equipment which might clank or rattle. They rode silently, single file, to a concealed spot near the compound of the enemy clan, then dismounted and left the ponies with a few holders. (Kareen on both occasions was one of the youngest men, and therefore assigned to look after the horses.) The older fighting men crept silently into positions overlooking the entrance to the enemy clan compound, and settled into concealment, aiming rifles at the gate. The Pathans usually send a woman out first every morning, but she would be ignored. The first man to exit, however, is shot by EVERYBODY, the shooters then dashing to their ponies to gallop away home!!!

Mr. Bacha Afridi was something of an autodidact, and knew a LOT about Numerology. After a long series of calculations, the letters of my name were declared to be a VERY powerful numerological combination. Or perhaps Bacha fibs thus to everyone for whom he does the analysis.

Making Boards the Hard Way

Temporary Road Repairs

We decided that we had waited long enough for the road to Gilgit to be passable, and purchased two seats in a 4-wheel-drive open jeep which would drive north as far as it could possibly go. At that point maybe we would be able to walk over the still-blocked section and reach Gilgit. The jeep skidded off the washed out road three or four times that morning and needed assistance to get it moving again. The jeep crew and some local men repaired the road by fitting newly-cut pine tree trunks into areas which had been washed away by the rain and melt-water. In the evening a powerful storm whipped down the valley, chasing us into shelter from stinging sleet and occasional hail. Seemed the road was becoming **more** fully blocked, rather than less. And not one soul was met who had walked south across the long section of the road not yet passable. So Linda and I gave up on reaching Gilgit, and headed south again to explore the many other wonders of the Indian subcontinent.

Empty Naran Youth Hostel

Photo by
Linda hill

Hardy
Goatherds

In Naran we opened up another Youth Hostel for the season, but the warden got 'creepy' with Linda, earning an abrupt telling-off for his slimy efforts. We did finally get the hang of making our own chapatis there, using nothing but coarse flour and water, so we ate a very satisfying, hot, filling meal. A government tourist official came to the youth hostel and recruited us to play Farangi hikers in a promotional film he was shooting. We spent most of one morning, wearing our backpacks, and marching always uphill while his camera rolled.

Our favorite lodging in Abbotabad soon re-welcomed us. No-one had lodged there in the nine intervening days.

Lahore's Red Mosque

Riding busses most places in Pakistan we were witness to some extremely stupidly dangerous stunts pulled by the drivers. It always froze my blood to hear the driver, after VERY narrowly avoiding a head-on-collision with a massive lumber truck, say

"Ensh Allah", which means "God Willing" in Arabic. The driver, rather than take responsibility for his own safety, just drives stupidly and puts it all in the hands of Allah whether or not he and his passengers will survive.

The Railways of India

We crossed the border into India easily on the train. Once past border formalities I was annoyed to learn that watches needed to be set ahead by 30 minutes, which caused us to just miss our connecting departure to Amritsar. We settled down to kill 3 hours by ordering a nice Thali meal at the station restaurant. Thali is a well understood system which on the railways uses a small, rather heavy steel tray with various separate compartments pressed into the tray. The larger central compartment will contain a dollop of rice, with the surrounding locations each containing a different spicy condiment. Sometimes bread or chapattis are also included. Then each diner selects a mix of condiments and adds them to the central rice, mixing as appropriate, and carrying scooped bites to one's mouth with the right hand.

Another big advantage to the Rail system in India is that any decent sized town station includes a restaurant where travelers know the food will be reliably good, and extremely good value. On long train journeys a railway employee moves through the carriages taking orders for breakfast, lunch or dinner as appropriate. The meals are standardized, and one can order a vegetarian or a non-vegetarian 'Thali' meal. You pay a small fee and receive a written slip of paper. The railway employee debarks from the train at the next station, and telegraphs the orders ahead. Then in 30 minutes or an hour, covered carts board the train, being pushed up and down the length, with steel trays being exchanged for chits. Similarly, the covered carts reappear to pick up the dirty trays and carry them off to be cleaned and re-used.

The Indian railway system was astonishingly well run and efficient. Thousands of trains traveled their routes every day, and were overwhelmingly likely to remain on-time. The railways were the particular domain of a strong sub-culture of Anglo-Indian families, and it was said to be impossible to gain employment on the railroads without a Railway-Anglo-Indian pedigree.

The Indian railways also provide excellent entertainment. Plenty of performers spent their entire careers boarding passing trains, entertaining for tips in each sequential passenger car, then debarking and repeating the process in the other direction. In addition, it was understood everywhere that the wooden slat luggage racks above the seats could be repurposed as bunks for sleepy passengers. Train-riding Indians were generally very friendly, and desired nothing more than a long conversation with a low-budget tourist to their country.

Riding the rails, a team of six Indian students engaged me in conversation. One of the young men, however, was quite 'spacey' and his English was disconcerting. When he spoke up, the other guys out of his line of sight indicated to me that he might be a bit crazy.

"Pacific Ocean!"—"Stars!"—"Telephone Number!"—"Cool Drinks!", followed by the grim pronouncement which still occasionally haunts my dreams—"We get ice from the horses for our procedures!"

Punjabi Sights

Immediately noticeable when entering India from Pakistan is how much more colorful, social, and happy the women appear to be. One sees Hindu and Sikh ladies on every side, laughing and chattering merrily with one another. The Muslim ladies are forced to hide themselves and behave with quiet decorum.

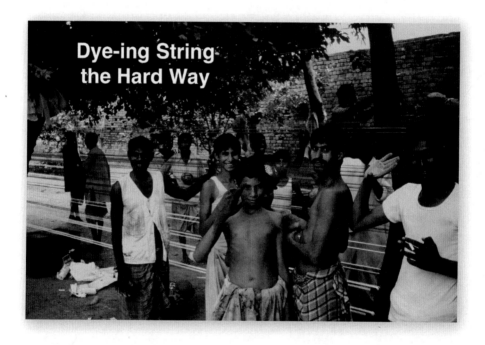

Dye-ing String the Hard Way

Not far from Amritsar we visited the Shalimar Gardens, which were nice, but not nearly as appealing as the gardens we visited later in Kashmir. Amritsar's Golden Temple, the mainspring of the Sikh religion is quite a satisfying experience. We entered, after being explicitly welcomed by some of the attendants, who showed us to a good place to sit, high on the stone "bleachers" above the lovely pond around the gleaming gold-leaf-covered temple. Pleasing live music emanated from two directions, and everyone seemed to be in a good, mellow mood. Soon after our arrival the temple attendants served everyone in sight a very nice light free meal of rice and spicy vegetables. It is a particularly wonderful place to spend an afternoon.

I had been dealing with intermittent dysentery for over a month already, feeling quite sick perhaps every other day, but this hadn't stopped me from traveling. To minimize the chance of catching something worse we never drank water except if we had witnessed it boiling as tea. For the same reason we made sure to never ingest a scrap of ice. Another handy source of 'safe' water was to purchase cucumbers, (for sale cheaply on every street), wash them, peel them carefully, and eat them in place of a glass of water. The Punjab region seemed to produce particularly tasty cucumbers.

Sikhs

The Sikhs still maintained a reputation for honesty, though this was starting to slip. Every armored truck guard or bank guard in that part of the world was Sikh.

From the Golden Temple we walked back to the railway station, and Linda bought 2 tickets north to Jammu. One of the advantages to traveling with a woman was that India railway stations maintained 2 ticket lines, one for men and another for women. The men's line usually resembled a trial by combat, as men in the Punjab, for some reason, just will NOT stand in a queue. Instead, it is necessary to sidle up towards the ticket window from the side, using one's elbow and one's physical strength to maintain and improve your position. The Punjabi 'fat lines' I found very annoying. The women's line usually consisted of one or two ladies at most. Much easier and more civilized to purchase tickets there.

The Vale of Kashmir

Riding to Jammu, we followed a sign saying 'tourist office' to a building where the staff rented each of us a piece of floor to sleep on for the rather high price of 2 rupees. Overnight the hard floor, heat, and mosquitoes all conspired to prevent really good rest. In the morning we bargained for a bus ride, and continued up the ridge by many switchbacks. At the summit a 4 km long tunnel spat us out into the lovely vale of Kashmir, but by then light was fading. Eleven hours on the hard bench seats of the bus was a trial.

In the bus depot of Srinagar, dozens of young men solicited us to stay on their houseboats, and we walked out with the most persuasive. A series of really gorgeous lakes surround Srinagar, and a houseboat holiday is an attractive option for middle-class Indian

Srinagar

Houseboat

families. We took a narrow shikara boat gratis across the lake and back to see more boats moored to the far shore. Finally we chose the boat belonging to "Uncle" and settled in to cook up some chapattis. Sitting languorously on the front deck that evening, a succession of craft-vendor boats lined up to come on board and display their wares in sequence. Jewelers were particularly thick, as were manufacturers of painted papier mâché boxes.

Both Linda and I went into Srinagar town to visit Jewelers who had briefly visited our houseboat. I had some pieces of Iranian turquoise mounted as rings for gifts. Linda was enamored of 'floppy' rings, with 30 or 40 jewels mounted separately and attached flexibly to the ring body, so that they rang and rattled against one another.

Foreigners as Targets

But something was amiss in the minds of the young Kashmiri Muslim boys. The day we arrived a boy had thrown a potato at my back, then run off. He missed me, but it seemed strange. This day, on a wide, muddy residential Srinagar street, a sticky clod of mud hit Linda in the small of her back. We both looked back along the empty road, and I was already moving fast when a young man's eye appeared around a shielding corner, getting very wide, then vanishing! He was running FAST, and I never did see him again, but knew exactly where he had gone by the people whose gaze was following him as he ran. I sprinted two blocks and two turns, the second into a narrow alley. I thundered past the woman who turned out to be his mother, and at the other end of the alley, a man looked into an open door in the wall, so I chased the little ratbag inside! Two children were looking up a set of crude stairs and were astonished to see a furious Farangi thunder up the stairs. I stopped at a locked wooden door at the top of the steps, and could not force myself to break through the door into the harem area. The father from downstairs came up behind me, tugging on my shirt-sleeve and speaking in a whining voice as I took huge breaths to recover my oxygen shortage. I pantomimed the crime of the hidden son, and his father pantomimed the swats on the bum that he would deliver. The violated couple led me downstairs and out of the hidden alleyway where Linda waited, wondering how many social taboos I had shattered.

The next day another Muslim boy hit me in the back with a mud-clod. After a short chase, I caught up with him, and gave the fellow a severe shaking, so that his teeth clacked together. I have never been able to figure out why in Srinagar, young boys thought that they should throw things at our backs and then run off. Linda was dressed as modestly as any of the local Muslim ladies. If any of you readers know what might have been the motivation, I'd love to hear from you.

Just Another Pilgrim on the Truck to Leh

The long-distance truck depot was not far from the Srinagar bus yard. I found a driver/owner who seemed cautious and sane, and bargained for two rides some way up towards remote, storied Ladakh ("Lah-DAHK"), also called Indian Tibet. We stayed there in Sonnamag two nights, then found a ride for only a dollar each all the way to Leh, the capital of Ladakh! The truck was carrying vegetables and we were encouraged to add some of the truck's vegetable payload to our dinner. That night our bed was on the macadam road in front of the truck (1 am to 5 am). It was a bit hard, but better than the ground off-road which was covered with fist-sized sharp rocks. We had to wait a long time for a very large convoy of Indian Army vehicles to pass. They carried supplies up to the army garrisons of Indian Tibet.

The town of Leh welcomed us with excellent cheap lodging at the Antelope hotel. We tried the DAK bungalow, but it was booked for the next 10 days by German bus tourists. We chatted with the Germans to discover that their ONLY topic of conversation was how much they had hated the long bus rides, and why didn't the government provide any air connections to Ladakh, anyway??? Those Germans were not allowing themselves to enjoy their adventure holiday in the least. The only airfield in Ladakh was the military one, though there were no aircraft squadrons stationed there. It seemed as though its purpose was to provide one more military option to the Indian force commander if Pakistan or China should try to conquer Ladakh.

Hindu Kush
Road Hazards

Hindu Kush
Village

Scenery in Ladakh was spectacular, with picturesque monasteries crowning many of the hilltops. Blindingly green strips bordered the seasonal river, frozen for eight months of the year, with barren moonscapes everywhere else. The local Tibetan-style costumes of the Ladakhi people were everywhere in evidence, but the local folks had learned to demand payment anytime a camera shutter clicked towards them, so I didn't take many good photos of exotic garb. Linda was more successful with her Single-Lens-Reflex camera which could take closeup photos at rather long distances. Many of the images I include in this narrative were snapped by Linda.

We had unwittingly arrived just at Leh's tourist HIGH season, as the famous festival at Hemis monastery (the largest and most important pilgrimage site in Ladakh) would begin in a few days, with festivities lasting nearly a week.

Ladakh Monastery

View from the Monastery

Ladakh Crowd

Ladaki Monks

Prayers

Our third morning in Ladakh we decided to visit a very photogenic monastery which we could see just down the river valley. We set off to walk there, but the unnaturally clear air in those high altitude vistas deceived us as to how far away our destination actually was. We reached the foot of the monastery hill after a six mile walk rather than the expected half-mile! Climbing up with a few locals to visit the monastery we spotted one of the package-tour busses arriving below, which disgorged 40 tourists. We were interacting with a really lovely young mother in her traditional dress, carrying her baby and her offering. When the other party caught up with us, they all deployed expensive cameras including 3 motion picture cameras to photograph her at close range. My heart was just about broken as all the newcomers treated her exactly as they would an animal in a zoo, filming, then turning away embarrassedly to continue the climb to the top of the monastery. When the package tourists had passed on by, our objectified young mother seemed disconcerted, and was no longer willing to interact with us.

Hemis Festival

The Hemis festival had no published plan of activities, so what might or might not occur on any given day was a mystery. We took an hour-long share-taxi ride the 40 miles from Lei on the most likely day and were gratified to find the demon-dances being performed. The first set of 4 demons wore skeleton-like costumes, and the second dancing contingent had devil-like masks and tunics. These used a sword to cut up a small humanoid doll which bled convincingly. Heavenly warriors later appeared to dance away all the demons.

Hemis Scene

Demons Dance

Demons Dance 2

Demons Dance 3

Hemis Procession

Hemis monastery was extensive, and built up to three stories tall, with every floor and roof and balcony sprouting local Ladakhi observers in lovely costumes. The major courtyard was big enough for people to cluster around all the sides and still have room in the center for the featured dances. The entire scene was colorful, otherworldly, and desperately fascinating.

When night fell, instead of returning to our lodging in Lei, we slept in a field outside the monastery along with plenty of the local pilgrims. The weather was clear, and bitterly cold, but my down sleeping bag, which I had carried for years, really came through as exactly the proper bedding. The stars were beautiful, and in the small hours of the night I saw a number of excellent meteors as they burned up over the Himalayas.

Our second day at the Hemis festival, nothing much seemed to be happening in the morning, and nobody had a clue of what might

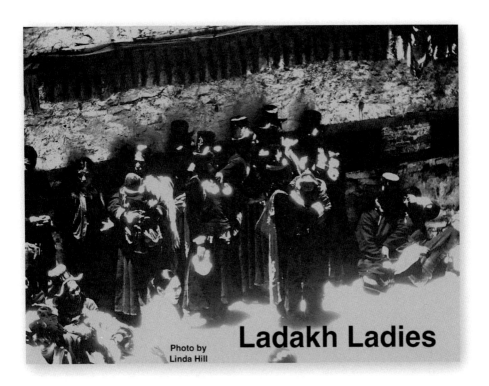

Photo by
Linda Hill

Ladakh Ladies

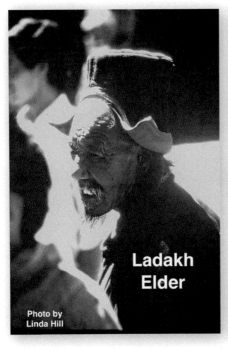

Ladakh
Elder

Photo by
Linda Hill

Traditional Dress
Photo by
Linda Hill

be scheduled for the afternoon and evening. We returned to Lei by share-taxi, buying several liters of Chiang, a locally brewed corn-based alcoholic beverage, decanted into re-used plastic soft drink bottles. The process of buying the Chiang included sampling a small glass of the stuff from each of various women promoting her own batch of brew. Chiang tasted rather yeasty and boring at first acquaintance, but was increasingly yummy as the evening progressed, and the inebriation level rose.

Ladakh Village

To the Hill Station

We were sad to finally leave the Ladakhis behind, but our curiosity was for the time being satisfied. Linda and I rode trucks back down through Srinagar, Jammu, and then back up into the foothills to a hill station called Manali. The multiple-day journey seemed even longer coming back than it had seemed climbing up.

We Rode and Slept under this Truck

I had always wanted to visit Dharamshala, the capital of the Tibetan government-in-exile. That remote town hides way up in a different section of Himalayan foothills. When we visited, the Dalai Lama himself was touring elsewhere, but we were welcomed at the multi-day funeral ceremonies of a minor Lama.

The full force of the Indian summer heat then held the plains in its crushing grip. Historically, every year in the heat before the monsoon breaks, all of the Indian government officials move their offices and families up into pleasant areas of the Himalayan foothills, leaving only a handful of the lowest seniority men to stand watch in the stifling plains. Linda and I decided to spend the time before the monsoon in the foothills, rather than go immediately to Delhi. A few other backpackers loitered around Manali for the same purpose.

The top floor of a lovely roomy bungalow was rented, a mile outside of central Manali. Surrounding the property were many acres of hemp fields. Fresh green hemp plants were the most common plant to appear in any patch of uncultivated land.

Two days after arrival, the nearby bungalow was rented by a family from the plains of India. It became clear that those folks had never really traveled away from home before. They succeeded in bringing the Indian slums with them up into the Himalayan foothills. That family spent all day and half the night shrieking loudly at one another, shattering the pristine quiet of the mountains. They threw all of their trash out the windows of their building onto the clean, well-tended lawn below, and swept any additional dirt and trash down on top of the mess. None of our little community of locals and Farangi could believe the horrible, inconsiderate behavior.

After only a week of relaxation the monsoon broke, resulting in LOTS of rain where we were. The deluge was of such magnitude that it washed the mountain roads out, dropping sections of the road into the valley below, and dropping rocks and debris onto the road at other locations. This meant that we could not leave Manali. The town was so small that it did not boast of a bank, therefore there was no way to change traveler's checks for spendable rupees, and we had completely expended the stock of currency we had brought along.

I had been dealing with low-level bacillary dysentery for a few months, and it now took me down hard. The Manali Mission Hospital diagnosed my dysentery, prescribing antibiotics as well as a chalky white medicine delivered in a big opaque brown-glass bottle. When informed that I had no money, the Mission Hospital treated me for free, and took pains that I would not feel guilty or bad about accepting their assistance gratis. My medicine bottle sat on the mantel above our fireplace, and I took a spoonful every morning and evening, but I was definitely not well.

Munchies

One evening Linda walked the mile into Manali town to have dinner while I remained at the bungalow, too sick to consider the hike, and not feeling hungry. I took down my nearly-empty medicine bottle to find that what remained was a sludge of powder and water. I swallowed my tablespoon, and soon realized that I should have all along been shaking that bottle before dispensing my medicine. I was flying, really doped up by the super-dose,

Monsoon Collapse

and also STARVING with an acute case of the 'munchies'. When Linda returned, well after dark, she was a good enough sport to accompany me back to town, discovering glowing caterpillars on the way, and walking a few inches above the earth, blasted by the beauty of the moonlight.

Once in Manali, only a single café was still open, and they could serve only a single dish of okra and HOT peppers. I do not think I have ever eaten anything so chili-hot, and I know I have never enjoyed any curried vegetable more.

Road Debris

There seemed to be no appreciable progress on re-opening the road from Manali to the plains, and my dysentery wasn't causing me too much grief. After 15 nights in Manali we decided to ride a bus as far as we could, then walk around the various impassable places in the road. Since we were completely out of money, I sold turquoise to get the rupees needed for travel. At the first blockage we walked up the steep hillside a few hundred yards to above the slide area, and across and back down to the road on the other side. The intermittent torrential rains did NOT assist with this stroll. There a bus was captive on the three-mile-long stretch of road between two impassable spots, but still had petrol. It carried us to the next blockage where we repeated the exercise. By nightfall we found ourselves a bus to the nearest big city. There we changed money and transferred on to Delhi.

Mahout Linda

New Delhi

We settled in to a guest house near the center of Delhi, a room on the second floor behind a wide, tiled patio. Due to the monsoon our room often flooded, because big leaves would quickly block the drain from the patio. We complained to the management, suggesting they must do something to avoid the twice or thrice daily room flooding. Their response was

"But in three weeks the Monsoon will be over!"

That short-sighted mode of thinking caused us to move to another guest house.

The most interesting places to visit around Delhi were Ashoka's Iron Pillar, the Taj Mahal, and Fatepur Sikri (FAH-teh-poor-see-KREE").

The Iron Pillar, over 1600 years old, and uncorroded, stands 24 feet tall in the courtyard of a ruined palace. Modern analysis of the iron found that the composition of the metal is similar to no other known Iron implement, from either ancient or modern foundries.

The Taj Mahal is only a short train ride downriver from Delhi. I expected it to be pretty, but the amazing construct really blew

Taj Mahal in the Distance

me away. The Taj Mahal is one of those rare sites which is somehow much more than just the sum of its features and location. Until one gets really close it is not apparent that the many slabs of white marble are carefully inlaid with delicate borders and patterns of semi-precious stone, invisible at any greater distance. If you are in India, do NOT miss the Taj thinking it is just another pretty building.

In the 1600s the Rajah of Delhi moved his court, and pretty much the entire city, to another location called Fatehpur Sikri. There he had a new city built, all with the same overall architectural design. But there was a problem at the new site procuring enough drinking water in the dry season. After only 14 years the court moved back to Delhi, and Fatehpur Sikri was abandoned. The abandoned city is remote enough that its stones were not carried away to build other edifices. The city still sits there, beautiful, ruined, and extremely picturesque.

Ruins of Fatehpur Sikri

Fatehpur Sikri

Lovely Arches

Lawnmower

In the city of Jaipur I found seven scrawny men squatted in a line across the narrow grass lawn of the palace. Each had a small, sharp sickle in hand which he used to carefully cut the grass, a few blades at a time, then slowly duck-walking forward a few inches to continue the task. I spoke with one of the guards about the Indian Lawnmower, asking why they hadn't purchased a push lawnmower, with which one man could do the job in $\frac{1}{10}^{th}$ the time. He smiled pityingly at the stupidity of my question.

"If we did, then six men would have no work."

Years later I told this story to Walt, my father, who did a quick mental analysis, then asked me a question I couldn't answer.

"Was it better to have six men with work at the price of six men's lives pointlessly wasted?"

Indian
Lawnmower

Parasite Diagnosis

I found that my right eye was very sore, and soon identified an inflamed welt running across my eyelid towards my nose. Continual sweat and seepage made the location swollen and annoying. I showed the problem to a cheap local MD who told me it was a parasitic worm, happily eating its way across my eyelid just under the skin (!) The medico was blasé about it, I wasn't happy.

"How do I know it won't turn inward and eat its way into my eyeball?"

"Do not worry, that will not happen."
"Well, what can I do to prevent such worms in future?"
"There is nothing you can do, you breathed in the worm eggs with the dust in the air."

I got some ointment which would theoretically kill the marauding parasite. A few days later it reached the edge of my eyelid and chewed its way up out of my eye socket. That was good as it was less sore and annoying there. Then the scruffy little worm bumped into the scar barrier across the bridge of my nose, and didn't want to continue in that direction. It turned 180 degrees and began chewing its way BACK across my eyelid, left to right!! About at the halfway point the wormicide cream finally took effect and killed the parasite, which my body then proceeded to absorb.

Astronomical Observatory

The Pink City

We visited Jaipur, finding the Sultan's celestial observatory to be quite interesting. All of his custom-made observation constructs covered a large field, each allowing the collection of accurate data for a single astronomical subject. Also in Jaipur we noted quite a few genuine cobra-charming performers. They were actually interesting enough for me to justify a tip for a photograph.

Udaipur and the nearby Ajanta Caves were visited, but did not impress. However we discovered a HUGE crudely-built Iron Cannon named "Fort Breaker" which captured my imagination.

Genuine
Snake Charmers

Huge Iron Gun

The sprawling city of Bombay showed us the fabled 'gateway to India', as well as the Elephanta Caves, with walls covered with ancient Buddhist murals.

Portuguese Asia

Stories from other vagabonds had painted the coastal enclave of Goa, previously a Portuguese colony on India's west coast, as a near-paradise. Tropical weather, a kind and gentle ocean, wonderful fruits, and European-inspired cheese, along with a very low cost of living, all beckoned travelers to settle down awhile and relax. We rented a large dirty house, with limited electricity and a kerosene stove, about 3 minutes' walk from the beach in a town named Colva. One of the first things we did was to pur-

Fishing Village in Goa

chase beautiful potatoes and cook them up with ZERO spices, just to finally be able to taste potato itself for the first time in what seemed like years.

Photo by
Linda Hill

Goan Fishwives

Another feature of Goa was the prevalence of "Pig Loos". Most outhouses worldwide are placed over a pit, but in Goa they sat on a 10" high concrete slab, with a slot cut out in the back. Any local pig, when it heard us come out the back door, RAN as fast as it could, as only the first pig would fit in the slot. The quickest pig would look up at us, grunting hungrily, and immediately eat any of our waste with considerable gusto. This took a bit of getting used to.

Colva was a fishing village and the big outrigger canoes brought their nets in to the broad beach every evening, when all the children and fishwives would help to pull the nets onshore and sort out the catch. The Goans were friendly to the Farangi vagabonds living in their midst, and seemed to enjoy having us around. Linda and I noticed that the various small 'junk' fishes were separated and sold very cheaply. And it seemed that prawns were considered just another junk fish. I asked the ladies if we could sort through the junk fish baskets and buy only the prawns. They were perfectly willing, and from that moment on, we had access to as many pounds of prawns as we wanted for only about 15 cents per pound!!

Rip Current

I came very close to foolishly throwing away my own life a few days later. I had been quite sick with dysentery for months, and settling down here in Goa for a rest was rapidly restoring my health and energy. Mid-day I went out to the beach by myself, and did some body-surfing. What I did not realize was that the beach had a rather strong rip current which could carry one off-shore. Also I did not realize how low my reserves of energy had fallen. The beach sloped gradually off into deeper water, then suddenly dropped away. I was swimming continuously toward the beach, but over 10 minutes of effort, it became clear that the beach was increasingly farther away. I looked around, but there was NOBODY else in sight on the beach. I was on my own and I had a long time to realize how foolish I had been to go bodysurfing unaccompanied.

My only chance appeared to be catching a wave and riding it far enough towards the beach to reach a depth at which I could stand up. Several sets of waves came through, but nothing big. Finally a set with two big following waves came in. I put every ounce of my remaining energy into swimming fast enough to catch those waves, and I succeeded with the final swell. However, when that wave dropped me out, it was still too deep to allow me to stand up, and the rip current was again moving me, now completely exhausted, out to sea.

To know how deep the water was below me I did a surface dive and found the bottom only about 10 feet down. I settled my feet into the sand and pushed myself off at an angle, towards the beach. That worked to move me a few more feet towards shore. I swam feebly while gathering my breath for another surface dive and another use of my big thigh muscles to propel me inland. After about eight iterations I could stand on the bottom with my nose above the surface, and knew that I was going to survive. It was a very great relief to not be somewhere hundreds of yards out to sea, awaiting my death through drowning.

We finally pulled up stakes and headed south through India towards Sri Lanka. I was intermittently debilitated with dysentery, but still able barely to travel on most days. Apparently tetracycline does not completely kill those bacilli, because my symptoms reliably reappeared three days after stopping the latest course of tetracycline.

Cow Courier

Dung Processing

Wild Asian Elephants

A group of playful young Hindu men teased us in the railway station with snickering comments and catcalls. I didn't really know what their problem was. At the exit gate one of these guys stood deliberately in front of Linda so as to rudely bump her shoulder hard with his own. That disrespect couldn't be allowed to stand, so I sidled up to him and whipped my own shoulder forcefully into solid contact with his, unexpectedly spinning him 90 degrees, much to the delight of his buddies.

We had good luck the day we visited the Nature Reserve at Kumali. The weather was perfect and we saw one of the world's last herds of wild Asian Elephants.

Sri Lankan Smuggling

In the textiles market of Madurai we went silk sari shopping. There was a chance to make a little traveling money by smuggling the highest quality silk Saris into Sri Lanka. In that country there were no mills which could weave a full-width sari, so all saris made in Sri Lanka had a prominent seam down the middle of them. It was much more elegant to wear a fancy sari without such a seam, and folks there were willing to pay a premium. I picked out three silk saris, one RED wedding sari embroidered with gold thread, plus green patterned and yellow patterned saris for fancy formal wear. Linda purchased one red wedding sari and two lungis, white cotton sarongs usually worn by Hindu men. I folded and rolled my contraband saris into a very tight cylinder which I then concealed at the center of my sleeping bag bundle.

The ferry to Sri Lanka departed a town called Rameswaram, but there was a problem when we tried to buy our 3rd class tickets. By local regulation, foreigners such as ourselves were only permitted to buy first class tickets. We talked and argued, but couldn't find any way around the rule. The top deck was exclusively for the use of first class passengers, but there were no controls over how many tickets were sold. Every bench seat in the 1st class deck was occupied, with plenty of other folks seated on their luggage.

Don't Mess with Linda (1)

A Sri Lankan man lay napping on a first-class bench. We awoke him, politely asking him to sit up so that we could sit down. He pretended not to understand, making dismissive gestures with his hand. I knew this would infuriate Linda, so I turned away to look out over the harbor. Linda raised up her backpack, with jagged ends where the aluminum frame had been broken off, above the selfish man and dropped it on his stomach!! He sat up IN A HURRY, looking flustered and embarrassed, at which point I quietly thanked him for his politeness and we sat down.

The ferry was delayed and didn't reach the Sri Lankan shore until 1 am, after the last connecting train had departed, so everyone on the ferry was stranded there after debarking. Linda talked her way into sleeping in the first-class railway lounge which was set aside for women. I found a place to sleep in the soft sand around the railway station. But there was a problem. Folks had been using that same soft sand as a latrine for many years. The heat had desiccated all of the fecal matter that I removed from under and around my ground cloth, but still, with the muggy heat and plentiful mosquitoes, I spent quite an uncomfortable night.

Late next morning we rode the train all the way to the capital city of Colombo. Sri Lanka is a beautiful country, but was experiencing some political unrest. The majority Sinhalese Buddhists were determined to pass more laws which discriminated against the minority Tamil Hindus. Those Tamils had been brought to Sri Lanka from southern India by the British plantation owners when they discovered that the Sinhalese weren't willing to work loyally and cheaply on their plantations.

Much of Sri Lanka's exports were teas from the beautiful tea plantations covering much of the hilly uplands of the island.

After checking out the central museums we headed up into the mountains to Kandy, the spiritual capital of the country. The climate there was very nice, and food was cheap and good. It happened that the avocado season was peaking, and they had a bumper crop. Everyone had just TOO MANY wonderful, rich, ripe avocados, and were willing to take ANY tiny price for them before they inevitably went overripe and rotten. For 2 and a half cents one could buy two huge avocados and a pint of government subsidized full cream milk, and thereby have a lovely breakfast.

Buyers in Kandy instantly snapped up the lungis and wedding saris. It was a few days more until a jewelry store owner purchased my pair of additional seamless silk saris for his wife and daughter.

Brown Star Sapphire

Some time earlier I had written to ask my family members if there was anything they might want me to purchase for them while I was traveling. My dear mother, Roberta, hesitantly wrote that for reasons she could not enunciate, she had always wanted a BROWN STAR SAPPHIRE. We relocated to the town of Ratnapura, the source of almost all of Earth's star sapphires, to shop for a brown colored stone. Everyone in Ratnapura has a mine in their back garden, dug straight down 30 or 40 feet to the layer of dense clay which contains the gems. Just about every local man has a few sapphires wrapped up in a handkerchief which he would be most happy to show you. There really is no other reason to visit Ratnapura except to buy sapphires at the best prices anywhere.

Everyone agreed that brown colored stones existed, but they were rare, which was not to say that they were valuable, because nobody desired that color. I put out the word on the street that I was in the market for a big, glorious brown Star sapphire. Our land-lady had two sons and three nephews in the sapphire trade, and was determined that I should purchase from one of her approved dealers. Third day knocking around Ratnapura the landlady met me coming in the door, so excited that she couldn't hold still. She had found the stone I wanted, of about eight karats, definitely brown, and with a well defined six-pointed star. It belonged to one of the nephews, but he couldn't be there because he was part of a football team which was competing that afternoon on the city commons. Her son put me on the back seat of his scooter and put-tered me down to the football game. I met the nephew between halves, and he was ready to dicker. We bargained briefly on eight occasions, every time the referees stopped the game briefly he would run to me on the sidelines, then run back into play when the game restarted. We finally reached agreement on a price, and I cashed travelers checks to make the purchase. Thereafter I carried the unusual stone in my passport pouch, next to my skin.

That night I was awakened by Linda shaking me. She was clearly upset, and once I had lighted a candle we both could see that her hands were covered in blood!! She had dreamt that a rat was eating her finger, but in the dream she couldn't move to prevent it. When awake enough, surely enough, a rat was found eating her fingertip while she slept!! At that moment I swore an oath of eternal vengeance on all rats. We monitored Linda's rat bite closely, and were relieved when the wound didn't seem to be infected.

Don't mess with Linda (2)

Returning north towards India, we visited Sirigiya, a ruined for-tress on top of a lone upthrust 600-foot rock surrounded by jun-gle. The path up and down was along and around the rock, with lots of people, single file, protected from falling by only a flimsy pipe railing. Since we carried our backpacks, I left Linda on a bench guarding our stuff while I climbed the steep path up, saw what there was to be seen, then descended. Linda then headed up while I spent some time sewing to repair my clothing.

Sigiriya Overview

After an hour a worried Sri Lankan couple hurried up to me saying "Your Wife! There is trouble!" I dropped everything and was up and running that direction, abandoning our luggage. At the foot of the stairs I found Linda GLARING at six young men who looked quite abashed. As Linda had descended, one of the guys following her down, had shown off for his buddies by bravely reaching over her shoulder to squeeze her breast! This infuriated Linda, and her assailant was certainly astonished when she spun around, punched him smack in the teeth, then headed back upstream into the posse, assaulting all the guilty parties as she encountered them. The Sri Lankan couple had fetched me

NOT to PROTECT Linda, but rather to calm her down!! I put an arm around Linda, who after delivering so much mayhem, could not be certain which of the six abashed young men had been the primary grope artist. Therefore I didn't need to thump anyone, and could confine my support to additional Glaring. None of the embarrassed perps would meet my eye. Odds are they never disrespected another foreign woman.

Smuggling Spices

Finally returning to India on the ferry, the entire ship smelled of cloves. It was permitted for each arriving passenger to import a kilo of cloves for his own consumption, and just about everyone had seized the opportunity. I had my kilo in the top portion of my backpack, and another contraband kilo secreted inside my tightly-rolled down-sleeping-bag. Immediately upon disembarking, several touts offered to buy my cloves, attempting two annoying scams trying to cheat me out of as much of my profit as possible. Each of these attempts was thwarted, and no touts were injured. I made a nice profit. Overall, smuggling three silk saris in and bringing two kilos of cloves out, my 3-week-long tour of Sri Lanka had decreased my available traveling money by only $2 USD.

Ahead of us remained so many fascinating sites on the Indian subcontinent! And ever since I was a child I had been determined to see Mount Everest by moonlight. We rode the Indian railways north towards Nepal.

Madurai temple was the biggest and most important Hindu temple in India, and really rewarded our attention. There were always two or three different processions or rituals in progress somewhere in the sprawling series of buildings. The elephant stables could be depended upon to entertain a visitor while the dozen elephants were bathed or fed, or repainted with religious symbols. Learned Hindu teachers lounged around, always ready to engage and proselytize non-Hindu foreigners. Much of the decorative art had a distinctly erotic nature.

Erotic Sculpture

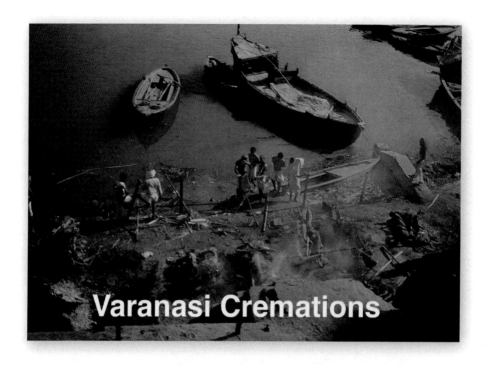

The holy city of Varanasi, on the Ganges, revealed its riverside Ghats to be filthy dirty, and always obscured somewhat by smoke from funeral pyres. Dedicated boats bring hundreds of tons of firewood every day to the burning Ghats. Hindus from all over the world wait in line with the remains of their loved ones to cremate them there. It is believed that if a Hindu's cremated ashes are submerged in the holy waters of the Ganges, the cycle of death and rebirth can be escaped, allowing the soul to immediately achieve nirvana. With colorful, amazing scenes at all hours of the day and night, the Ganges burning Ghats may be the best people-watching spot on Earth.

Ganges Barbershop

A lovely, shady tree stands at the center of a Buddhist shrine at Bodh Gaya. This is a direct descendant of the original Bodhi tree under which Gautama Buddha, 2500 years past, attained enlightenment. Particularly devout Buddhist widows spend their last days at Bodh Gaya, praying for the souls of their husbands.

Glass Bangle Seller

The Bodhi Tree

Buddhist Widows Photo by Linda Hill

My Most Foolhardy Act

Heading by rail out of Varanasi to as near as we could get to Kat-mandu, a young policeman told us that for our own safety, we must move to a half-carriage set aside only for tourists. He wore a new-looking uniform and carried a 4-foot-long bamboo stick called a 'lathi'. After realizing that he was both serious and deter-mined, we moved up the platform and into the designated car-riage. There were already four other backpackers collected there, and we did standard queries. The young cop sat beside me on the hard bench seat as we finally began the journey to Raxaul and opened conversation. He seemed miffed that I was not thank-ing him for protecting us all from the imaginary bad actors. My assurances that I'd been traveling all over India for eight weeks and had yet to experience any serious violence contradicted his own favorite version of the truth.

There were still plenty of empty seats in the 'tourist only' car, though the remainder of the train was quite crowded, every seat claimed and many people standing for the long journey.

As the train built up speed after the next stop, a small 'babu' (shopkeeper or clerk)-type man ran up at the last moment and slipped into the tourist half-carriage. My policeman stood up slowly, brought himself up to his full height, and marched over to eject the interloper. I watched as the short babu argued with the cop, obviously pointing out that he was no threat to the tourists, and that the only unclaimed seats remaining were here. And anyway, there were no doors between the carriages, so until the next station, there was really no way he could immediately leave. I lost interest and went back to my reading, becoming instantly completely absorbed by the prose of my paperback.

A few moments later my head snapped up to a changed scene. For some reason my policeman had lost patience with the babu, had pushed him down against the exit door, and with the lathi, proceeded to strike him repeatedly with a great deal of force! Whack, Whack, Whack!!

In a heartbeat I lost my temper, and launched myself ballistically. I reached the cop, snatched the lathi out of his hand, (it was tethered to his wrist), grabbed him by the shoulders, spun him around and SLAMMED him against the carriage wall, one hand under his chin raising him up until his toes could barely still reach the floor. I screamed into the policeman's terrified face, threatening horrible mayhem, flecks of my spittle coming to rest on his face and shoulders!!! Finally my ire subsided as I

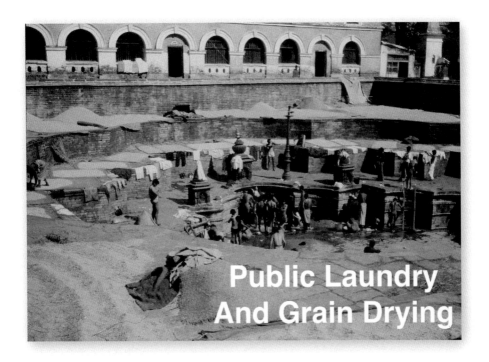

**Public Laundry
And Grain Drying**

Grain
Drying

Photo by Linda Hill

slid him back onto the floor, whereupon he scuttled out of the carriage onto the platform! The babu had also disappeared.

I walked slowly back to my seat as though in a trance, but shuddering with emotion. None of the other backpackers would meet my eye. I sat down heavily. Linda leaned in close to my ear and whispered,

"That was **REALLY STUPID**, Chick."

Ruefully, I could only agree. It would now be only a few minutes before the assaulted policeman reappeared with the local Special Weapons team to demonstrate to me that policemen must be treated with much greater respect than I had shown. There beside me on the seat was the cop's soft hat, awaiting his return.

To everyone's surprise, the hat lay there beside me for the next six hours until we descended at Raxaul. I don't really know how I came to be spared punishment. Perhaps my policeman felt that he had lost so much 'face' that he never wanted to see any of us again. Just chalk it up to very strong undeserved vagabond's luck.

Katmandu

Busses swept us up 5000 feet in five hours to Katmandu. The city itself doesn't much impress, but the setting, with snow-capped mountains all around, is fantastic. Katmandu in 1976 was a very dirty city. The locals thought it normal to defecate directly on the terraces of any of the temples or stupas in-town, and there was no service which might ever clean them up again. Our first-chosen lodging was in a guest house which fronted an abattoir in the street, and a motorcycle repair shop nearby. Awakened to the screams of dying pigs, interrupted by the screams of dying motorcycle engines convinced us to relocate to a quieter neighborhood.

Khatmandu Curbside Slaughterhouse

Food in Nepal was simple, but satisfying. Noodle dishes predominated, and every eating establishment included one or two vegetable choices. Storefront bakeries were very common, and two of these on the main road offered a new treat. Over the counter one could purchase delicious coconut macaroons decorated throughout with small black dots. The black inclusions were potent hashish, and a single macaroon was enough to send two backpack tourists flying for an entire afternoon.

From the capital we made two trekking excursions. The first was of two days hiking up and out along a mountain ridge, chosen just to see the lovely mountain scenery.

Wife Voice

While on our trek both Linda and I noticed something about Nepalese women. The girls' voices are invariably sweet and musical, but many of the older women croak and bark. We figured maybe it has something to do with smoking making the voices progressively more harsh and discordant. Then we bumped into a new bride, only married a week, in her 'married woman' costume. The grating shout she used in place of a voice was bitter, sharp-edged, abrupt and soul-crushing. Apparently there is an accepted 'married' woman's voice, and the sweet-voiced girls adopt it immediately when they wed!

Heavy rainstorms made the trek much more difficult, less fun, and less scenic, so we turned back earlier than we had at first intended.

Himalayan Pilgrimage

The second excursion was launched to coincide with the next full moon. This found us hiking uphill all day long to reach a lonesome tea house situated on a ridge with a great overview. We bargained for places to sleep on the teashop's board benches, and ate our macaroons as the sun set in the misty Khatmandu valley behind us. Arising then in front of us, illuminating a spectacular array of snow-covered Himalayan peaks, appeared the biggest, brightest full moon imaginable. Once the hashish kicked in all I could do was lie silently on my bench, emotionally blasted by the scene. Out there at the horizon, the locals pointed out gleaming Mount Everest. This moment fulfilled my pilgrimage to view the world's highest peak by moonlight.

If continued tales of super-low-budget vagabonding through Southeast Asia, Australia, Oceania and the Far East are of interest, they will be detailed in the 3rd and final volume of this 'Just Another Pilgrim' series of travelogues.

Many thanks, gentle reader, for persevering through to the wrap-up of this volume of my memoir. I am sure that if we had known one another, you would have proved an excellent companion on those travels.

Chick Lewis

Preview of
Just Another Pilgrim on the Boat to Wewak

Returning to my cheap lodging of a Bangkok evening, I was confronted by a uniformed policeman and another man who spoke good English. They backed me into the recessed entranceway of a closed shop, between the display windows, blocking my path back to the sidewalk. The cop glowered at me menacingly, while his brother-in-law announced:

"We know you have been messing around with drugs, and we are taking you to prison."
"Nah," I replied, "you've got the wrong guy."
"We know you have been messing around with drugs, and we are taking you to prison."
"Nope, that's not me!"

I had discovered from similar situations in the past that if one escalates the confrontation from the verbal to the physical, then the shakedown artists usually laugh and claim they had only been kidding. So I put my hand between the two, turned my shoulders to the side, and moved forcefully towards the street. Their faces got really ugly, and they both jammed themselves together, pushing me to a halt. The cop's hand went to the grip of his holstered revolver!! I had badly miscalculated. These guys were SERIOUS, and I would need to treat them with much more respect to avoid imprisonment.

Sources

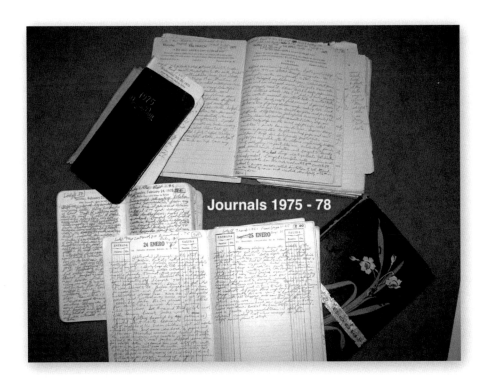

Journals 1975 - 78

Made in the USA
Middletown, DE
31 January 2024

48808983R00122